Memphis-Nam-Sweden

Memphis
Nam
Sweden

The Story of a Black Deserter

by Terry Whitmore

as told to Richard Weber
with an Afterword by Jeff Loeb

UNIVERSITY PRESS OF MISSISSIPPI / *Jackson*

First published in 1971 by Doubleday & Company, Inc.
Copyright © 1997 by University Press of Mississippi
Manufactured in the United States of America

00   99   98   97   4   3   2   1

The paper in this book meets the guidelines for permanence and durability of the Committee on Production Guidelines for Book Longevity of the Council on Library Resources.

Library of Congress Cataloging-in-Publication Data

Whitmore, Terry.
    Memphis, Nam, Sweden : the story of a black deserter / by Terry Whitmore as told to Richard Weber ; with an afterword by Jeff Loeb.
        p.   cm.
    Previously published: Garden City, N.Y. : Doubleday, 1971.
    ISBN 0-87805-983-0 (cloth). — ISBN 0-87805-984-9 (paper)
    1. Vietnamese Conflict, 1961–1975—Personal narratives, American.
    2. Vietnamese Conflict, 1961–1975—Desertions—United States.
    3. Vietnamese Conflict, 1961–1975—Afro-Americans. 4. Whitmore, Terry. I. Weber, Richard P. II. Title.
    DS559.5.W48   1997
    959.704'38—dc21
    [B]
                                                                    96-29608
                                                                         CIP

British Library Cataloging-in-Publication data available

*For all our brothers—black, white and yellow—
who have had enough and long for the day
when they can live like civilized human beings*

CONTENTS

FOREWORD

The casualties from the American devastation of Vietnam will probably never be fully reckoned. For the people of South Vietnam, it now appears to be an end to their land and to their race. To the general American consciousness, the casualties are only just beginning to encompass more than body counts.

Terry Whitmore was a near-casualty of that war, an ordinary guy—a brother from the block, as he'd say—who was forced by an unusual chain of circumstances to extraordinary actions in order to salvage himself as a human being.

As tens of thousands of America's young men and women reverse the historic flow of immigration by fleeing from their homeland to peaceful refuges and new lives, Terry's story gains in significance. He is not merely one guy with guts enough to say "No" and head for a new country; he is in many ways an embodiment of this new wave of American emigrants. His story, however, is more exciting than most and laced with a sense of humor that is sadly lacking with many of his counterparts.

There is small chance of Terry's story "waking up" the American people. But I trust that it will offer hope and another possible alternative to those young Americans who are searching and wandering.

To my lovely wife, Elizabeth, I offer my gratitude for her patience and assistance in the writing of this book. And thank you to the score of sympathetic individuals who have given me their advice and encouragement.

Richard Weber

Stockholm, Sweden
August 31, 1970

MEMPHIS
          NAM
              SWEDEN

BACK HOME

"I'm gonna kill you."

My own brother. My own goddamn kid brother is coming at me with a knife.

"I'm gonna kill ya, ya big bully!"

The kid is not bullshitting. He has a big kitchen knife, and behind those tears in his eyes, he has a no-jiving look that can only mean "I'm gonna kill ya."

"Listen, jerk, don't be scaring me with no knife."

"I'm gonna kill ya."

That overgrown shitass wanted to watch cartoons and I wanted to watch an old flick on the family's one tube. So I bounced him off the floor a few times. Knocked his head up against the wall before being able to watch my flick. And the little jerk got angry! So pissed off that he came at me with a knife. He was big for twelve, but I managed to knock that knife out of his hand and whip his ass but good. Of course, my mother came home for that part of the action.

"Ma, he came at me with a knife!"

"My Ronnie? Never!"

Family life. Loved it. Eighteen years of shouting and loving . . . sports on the block . . . riding slick and balling chicks . . . in the black ghetto of Memphis, Tennessee. My home.

I don't suppose that fighting with kid brothers is anything unusual in any family. Except that in my family I was the oldest boy with too damn many kid brothers. So who caught all the shit when it hit the fan?

"Terry! Get up in that tree and get me some whippin' sticks."

Ever hear of digging your own grave? Well, I had to climb that goddamn elm tree, risk breaking my neck so I could pleat my own whip. My mother had one hell of a sense of justice. Everything short of my beating myself.

"Not that one, it's too small."

"But Ma . . ."

"You got yourself up there, boy. Now get back down here with some whippin' sticks."

I'd try my best to stay up in that elm tree the whole day, but eventually I had to come down. And Ma would be waiting to give me what I usually had coming to me. Not that my kid brothers were so innocent. They'd be watching from around the side of the house.

"Bend over them steps."

Funniest fucking thing those little jerks ever heard. Laughed their asses off while I got my ass whipped bent over the back steps.

My old man's idea of discipline was a little warped—when he bothered with it at all. Once when I came running home to him for a little comfort, he sprinkled cayenne pepper over my cut knee. First and last time. That pepper burned a lesson into my young ass: Never go crying to my old man again.

Ma ran the family. Dad brought the bread home, but Ma handled it. She had the education. A high school graduate, she could read and write. More than a lot of people on the block were able to do.

But my old man. Well, he loved the booze. Boozing with his buddies—that was his idea of living. Still, he managed to hold down the same good job for nineteen years. A metalworker. No matter how many times he was too hung over to show up for work, they'd never fire him. He was too good. So Ma got a steady paycheck from him. Plus the spare change he'd pick up around the block by fixing people's old cars and washing machines, which on my block were always breaking down. He never had any training at it. But he was good enough to get them working again. So when he was straight enough to do it, my old man had plenty of work.

"You sober enough to drive me to the store today?"

"Walk, goddamnit."

"In that case, Terry can drive me."

Now that would give my old man the ass. Not only was I too young to be driving, but he was the one who had taught me to drive so I could get him home in one piece after drinking with his buddies.

Pa could never argue with my mother. She was always right and had the last word. But when it came to bullshitting bill collectors, he was a goddamn artist. He'd be dumb enough to buy the shit on credit in the first place. Then he'd weasel his way out of paying the bills for months after they were due. Those bill collectors caught so much bullshit and grief, they'd settle for less just so they wouldn't have to come around to see him anymore. My old man even told off the FBI when they came around looking for me. Said they had no right to send his black boy back to the Nam while white boys were coming home. Threw the FBI right the hell out of our house.

But Ma was a God-fearing good American. When she wasn't breaking her back to run our family, she was at her church. After our family, religion was the biggest thing in her life. Her church was the Zion Temple. The jumping Saints. She was originally a Baptist, but that church was too social for my ma. The Baptists were all small-time businessmen and politicians on the make—so their churches were always after coins. And, of course, their reverend wore Stetson shoes and one-hundred-fifty-dollar suits. Whatever year it was, he had the car. None of this Ford or Chevy crap—only a Chrysler would do for the reverend. Ma didn't dig that.

The Saints were more religious. Singing, hand clapping, really getting carried away with their faith. They were simple people and poor. My mother felt good there. She even had me going to their Sunday school before I graduated from high school.

"You should at least be going to Sunday school. I'd like you to stay for the church service. But if you feel like you have to go, nobody is forcing you to stay."

Sunday school by itself was hard enough to make. At the

Baptist church, I'd just show up for roll call and then split for the malt shop. If my mother checked, they'd cover for me. None of that shit at the Zion Temple. The Saints didn't jive around with their religion. So there I was—the big-time athlete and Romeo from Lester High School—duded up at a Sunday school. Those kids gave me some weird looks. Like I was the whore in a convent. Ain't good enough for you? That's all I had to hear. Busted my ass to learn that bible and graduated as valedictorian. They even had me giving bible stories in church. That's when I learned that I could talk to people. I had the gift to rap like hell.

"That's Sister Whitmore's son up there. What a bright boy!"

My ma was about to bust out with pride. Her son was the star of the Zion Temple. I wasn't exactly ashamed of it myself.

But I just couldn't handle too many of those church services. Knock-out stuff. The Saints' reverend was loved for his shouting and screaming. He could carry on wailing for an hour and his voice would never crack.

"Look at that! Look . . . your mama's about to jump up screamin'!"

"Shut up. That ain't my ma."

We'd be eyeballing the whole scene from the back of the church.

"There she is! Your mama's jumpin' up."

"Don't look, man."

"I see your ma. Look at her! Goddamn, she's jumpin'."

"Shut up or I'll punch you, man! Don't look at my ma."

If we did make it to church, we'd place bets on how many times whose mother would jump up for a little soul shouting. But the Baptists were even worse. They'd have women fainting all over the church. Once the deacons even got to swinging out on the stage, and the police came to break up the fight. The Saints had their singing and shouting, but they were good, simple, down-home people. Ma felt good with them. And I guess I did too.

GROWING UP BLACK

When you're little, you never think about the fact that you're black. It just doesn't occur to you that you are colored, because you are around black all the time. Whenever you see a white man, he is either the milk man or the insurance man or in other words somebody who is coming around for money. Sometimes it was a white woman, the Avon lady peddling cosmetics. Coins —this is the only reason to see white people. Otherwise you are in your own neighborhood and this is your whole world. To hell with the people on the outside.

In school you start to grow, to get fucked up. Although you never really think seriously about it, you are always reading what the white man did in history—that is, American history. But while you are reading all this shit, you never see anything about brothers. Then you begin to sense something strange. Where do we come into the picture? What the fuck am I doing here? But you can't spend too much time thinking about it as a kid, because you're too busy growing up—growing up in your own neighborhood, that's what counts. The block and everything on it. Sports, just running around, and then girls. The problems in the outside world never penetrate. They don't mean a damn thing to you when you're growing up in your own neighborhood.

But when you reach high school, you have to go outside the neighborhood to work. This is when you really start to feel it. They do hate us. Just plain hate us.

My first part-time job as a kid was in a grocery store that was located in a white neighborhood. One of the guys who worked with me was white. We would always be messing around together, bullshitting and joking. He was from Mississippi. We worked in the back of the store where the goods came in. Carry in boxes, tear them open, stack all the shit on the shelves. One day we got a shipment of ladies' hair cream which I had to unload. There was a beautiful blonde broad on the cover of each of these boxes. I don't remember exactly what I said in reaction to this babe, but it was something like, "Man, I wouldn't mind having her!" To which this white cat replied, "If she were black, you *could* have her."

Well, that really knocked the shit out of me. I was hurt, but I couldn't say anything, no matter how mad I was. And I was furious. But you just don't let it come out. You keep it down, because you have to mingle with white people every day. So I kept my mouth shut, trying to overlook the problem. You had to do this to stay friendly with a white guy. And I did. But when one of them makes a wisecrack, you want so badly to knock him on his ass . . . you know that you can't. So you don't.

When I left the block, the word "nigger" was probably the most popular name the brothers had for each other. We always used the word "nigger" when talking to another brother. But as soon as we went outside the neighborhood and started fooling around with some white guys, none of that "nigger" shit was allowed. A white ass would be kicked but good if he said "nigger" to one of us. A line had to be drawn somewhere. And that kind of shit just didn't bounce.

I had another job at a Holiday Inn, where I experienced even more racial hate from the people who stayed there. A lot of them came up from the really Deep South. One night we, the bellboys and I, were sitting around the lobby, just shooting the bull. In came this drunk, a real cracker, looking for a room. But we were full up and apologized to him for it. Then I turned around and continued to talk to my buddies, one of whom was a white guy, just a guest from up North.

But this drunk wouldn't take no for an answer and started in with "goddamn motherfuckin' nigger, you listen to me when I'm talking, ya hear!"

At this, the white guy from up North shouted, "Shut up, you

bastard!" At first, I wasn't going to do anything but ignore it. I didn't want to get fired. But this other brother and the white cat went busting out the door after that cracker drunk who was now heading for his car. So I figured, let's straighten this dude out. While he was pulling out of the driveway, we were flinging stones at his car—little white stones from the base of the flagpole. Screaming "motherfucker" all the time.

But that was rare. We usually tried to ignore the problem while we were working and still in school. Sure we heard about the riots, SNCC, the black preachers and so on. But most of us just thought: "Fuck 'em. I wanna get ahead, so I can't be part of all that shit."

Whenever we came in contact with white men, we tried not to discuss the problem with them because we were afraid of losing our tempers, of going mad. We would talk about anything *but* the race problem. We thought that each one of us could make it on his own. Screw movements. We didn't need them then. But it couldn't work out that way. It was like trying to climb a staircase. Up one step, meet the man, fuckin' nigger, and then get kicked down a whole flight.

The most frequent contact we had with racists was with white guys cruising around town in their cars. We learned fast never to be caught waiting for a bus late at night in any neighborhood but our own. I had to take one home every night from the Holiday Inn motel. And it was the same shit almost every night. "Black motherfucker," and off they'd go. But sometimes they would pull up slowly; then you'd better make yourself part of the nearest telephone pole, because something was coming out that car window and you were the target. Usually it was warm piss in bottles. That would give us the ass. After a piss attack, we would always take it out on the next white driving through our neighborhood. Knock out a few windows, flatten a few tires, but we never really hurt anybody.

Of course, the cops would come around after one of these attacks. Dogs, black mariah, the works. It made no difference whether the guys they picked up were involved or not. If the

white dude said you did it, you did it. The cops would drive up
alongside a cat. "Get in the car."

"For what?"

"You broke his windows, that's what."

"I ain't done nothin'."

"Shut the fuck up, nigger, and get in the car."

You're in the car fast—and then you're in jail.

We spent a lot of time hanging around the launderette. It
had a front door and a back door. The man comes in the front;
we had it up out the back, and vice versa. For some strange reason, they never used both doors at the same time. So the
launderette was a good place to sit and bullshit. We never did
anything, just sit there and bullshit. It was our meeting place,
but the man was always busting in. It seemed as if there was no
place outside our homes where we could sit and bullshit and
not always be on the lookout for the man—because he was always
there. Always. And if you didn't do anything and said, "I ain't
moving," the other guys would think you were crazy. "Look,
nigger, you better run. They gonna kick your black ass no matter what you ain't done."

The worst ass-kicking I ever saw done by the man was to
this football player, James, who had his back busted playing
college ball. Some asshole had turned in a false alarm that
night. The fire department came, but no fire. Then the cops
came. James was the first poor bastard they saw. Now James's
mother was a schoolteacher, so James was not about to take shit
like the other guys do. I guess he was a badass too. James had a
brace on his back, so he couldn't run even if he had tried.

"Come over here, motherfucker."

"I ain't no motherfucker."

"C'mere, boy."

"I ain't no boy and you not supposed to be talking to me like
that."

"You ain't goin' nowhere now, smartass." Slammed him up
against the car. He couldn't move with this brace on his back.

Handcuffed one arm to the door handle. Then they took their clubs and just beat the living shit out of James. He tried, but he couldn't move. He just kept screaming that his back was broken.

James went off to the hospital. His mother raised beaucoup hell. But nothing happened. She was helpless. We expected it. We knew that you can't do anything but run when the man comes around. Guilty or not, brace or no brace, you just had it up. Split.

And that's mainly what it's like when you grow up black. You can never get back at the man. I think that's why years ago so many black cats became professional boxers. Then you can kick the shit out of the man and he can't do anything but watch. Otherwise you just have to had it up. Split.

RUNAWAYS

Cliff. About five feet five, a real stubby dude. One of my closest friends on the block.

We were watching TV one night over at his house while my other buddy, Bobby, was working at the drive-in as a carhop. Picture went off about ten o'clock. Then there's the news. Blahsie, blahsie about what's going on in the world. Oh fuck this shit, man, we're going out.

So we went outside, but we had nothing to do as usual. A train ran directly by his house and we headed towards it. We were going to cross the track to see Irma Jean. She's our pride and joy. Everybody's girl friend. Well, not everybody's girl friend. More like a pal, our buddy. She never went on about you don't do this, you do that. There were no love relations or anything like that. We were just close to her, even though she was a girl.

Her house wasn't too far. Just had to get over this huge parked train. Now we're sitting up there, just staring at it. It was tempting. We had planned to run away from home a long time ago. I did once, but it didn't work.

Fuck it. We started to cross the tracks. Didn't feel like waiting all night for it to move, so we climbed over this open coal car. Over and into it.

The engine started way up front. You know how trains start off chung, chung, chung all the way down the line. Chung—it jerks the car we're in. My first reaction was to hop off immediately. "No, let's ride it down to the big viaduct." O.K.

So we're sitting on the train as it pulls off slowly, just watching the scenery. The viaduct was about 150 yards away and we could see it coming. And we're going to jump off this thing when we reach the viaduct, so we can walk back up the track. Shit—

the viaduct went like sshhooong—gone! The goddamn train had picked up that much speed in just 150 yards.

Cliff is yelling at the top of his voice, "What? What the hell? Let's get off, man. Let's get off!" And I'm thinking, "What the fuck we gonna do?" This train is sshhooong. And he's screaming. These telegraph poles are whizzing, flying by. Goddamn, I can remember that fool putting one leg over the side with those poles flying by so fast. "No man, I'm coming back in one piece." So we just sat down in one little corner of the car. The poles flying by.

We're sitting there now, watching the scenery, watching the moon. The moon was supposed to help us keep our sense of direction. We got lost, of course. While we're watching it, that goddamn moon is playing checkers, jumping all over the sky. Back to the scenery. We watched these little country towns. Every fifteen minutes, the train passed through a country town which was so small and the train was going so fast, we could only see two or three lights fly by.

After a while, Cliff comes on an idea. "I wonder if I jump up on this end of the car, would I come down in the other end of the car?" He gets these weird ideas.

"I dunno man. Go ahead, try it." So I move to the back and he's going on like a kangaroo, up and down in the air. But every time he goes up, he comes down in the same spot. "There's something wrong, man. I'm not moving."

Finally we went to sleep for a while. We didn't have coats, just casual clothes. And only fifty cents in my pocket. That's all I had. Cliff had no money.

Early that morning—we didn't have a watch, so we weren't sure of what time it was—the train slowed down. Cliff says we're going to jump off this fucker, it's slowing down. I've never been jumping off trains. I didn't know anything about it. But Cliff knew about this shit. He had been living all his life riding trains around Memphis and jumping off. "C'mon man, let's jump." O.K.

So he flops over the side as the train is slowing down and

starts running alongside. Crash—I heard him land on a pile of rocks. Goddamn lucky I wasn't hanging over the side; I'd be a bowl of mush now.

I'm still between the cars, getting ready to jump—flatfooted. Of all the dumb things to do, I jump flatfooted. Hit that ground and all I can remember is turning somersaults over the rocks. Thank God I played football and had enough sense to roll as I feel. "Whit, you all right?"

I looked up out of the corner of one eye, "Yeah, I guess I'll live." My trousers are ripped, in shreds. My arms are scratched, bleeding. But Cliff's fine.

O.K., what are we going to do now? Start back down the fucking track to Memphis. That's all there is to do.

It's early morning and we walk on for about an hour. Getting nowhere. "We gotta get off this track and find a highway, so we can hitch our way home."

Cliff says no, keep on the track. "Look, man, fuck the track. We don't know how the hell far it goes. There might even be snakes hiding around here. We're out in the boonies now, man." Snakes. In the boonies. That sent us out hunting for two huge sticks to club the snakes which just had to be hiding there.

No snakes, but we do come across a dirt road. I want to take this just to get us off these tracks. Off we go, searching for someone who knows where the hell we are and how to get away from it.

We spot a mobile home with a few people sitting out front. They're white. So we get a bit frightened. "Look, man, we better not go up there." "But we only want to know where the highway is." Fuck it. We go.

Now here are these white people sitting in their front yard just before dawn, minding their own sweet business. And along come two black cats walking up with clubs in their hands!

We walk up tall. I let Cliff take the lead. They're all giving us the hairy eyeball, but no one is saying a word. Eeek! The broad lets out a scream and runs into the trailer. Oh shit, we done for now! The two dudes spring to their feet. Cliff starts to give them the let's-be-friendly rap. Poor Cliff, he used to stutter a lot.

"L-l-look, look, I wanna n-n-n-know wh-where the highway is." Clifford has his club down between his legs and I'm looking like Paul Bunyan with mine on my shoulder, still standing tall. This white dude is having the shits about now. He doesn't know what the hell to think. The other guy walks over to his car to get something from the trunk. Now what?

The dude is obviously pissed. "The highway? What goddamn highway you talkin' about?"

"Yeah, the highway. We looking for the highway. Ya see, we're lost. We don't know where we are now and we want to find the highway."

"I'm gonna show you where the goddamn highway is. You turn your little asses round and go right back where you came from." Sweet pleadin' Jesus, what did we run into this time!

The big guy walks over to Cliff like fucking Zorro or somebody, reaches down fast, grabs his club and backs off. "What the hell you doin' with this, boy? What you want around here?"

"Look, mister, that's just to kill snakes with."

"Don't give me that shit, boy. I know what you're up to. Now you move your asses outa here, ya hear me, boy!" Say no more.

"Cliff, let's move." But I'm not about to turn my back on this dude with Cliff's club. Then I spot the other dude at the car. "Cliff, look out. He's got a gun!" The son of a bitch was pointing a gun at us and screaming away.

"Run, ya li'l bastards, 'fore I blow your balls off!" Holy shit, that wasn't nothing but the fucking word then. We had it down that road.

Why, I don't know, but these clowns came after us in their car. All we could see were their lights coming up fast behind us. Cliff hit the corner and dove into the bushes. I went right over his head and into a berry patch. That shit was eating my ass up, sticking the hell out of me but good. But I was too scared to move.

When the car reached the curve, it stopped. Shining their

headlights around, looking to get us. The stickers are still doing a job on me, but I ain't making a sound. They gave up soon and drove off. Cliff pulled me out and we hit the tracks again. Still have my club. Still looking out for those snakes.

We never met any snakes, but we did come across some dogs. A whole pack of these mangy mongrel mutts. Maybe they were supposed to be guarding the tracks, because one hound started to go crazy. *Ahroo, roo, roo.* "Just keep walking. Pretend you don't see them." Cliff's full of bright ideas.

Another one starts in. Then five or six more join them. *Ahroo, roo, rooo.* And these are big fucking dogs! They're moving up on us, right onto the tracks. I'm squeezing that club. Here comes my big chance.

When we stopped walking, the dogs would stop running. They'd just walk on slowly, but closer and closer. We were scared. Sure, I have my club, but like I said, these are big dogs.

A train whistle. A train was coming. Whoooo! Those dogs knew how to get off that track when the train came. We ran alongside it until we felt that we were way the hell away from those hounds. And then we ran some more.

The sun was coming out. We felt a little better, safer, closer to home. Little did we know that we had gone as far as the bor-derline between Kentucky and Tennessee. All we knew was that we were coming to one of those country towns that flew by the night before. It was a weird little country town. No brothers anywhere. A nice sunny morning in some hick town, ladies in their long dresses coming to shop, men in coats and ties. And no brothers. "Whit, this sure is a funny place."

"Yeah, I was just thinking the same thing." Maybe if we saw a brother, we could ask him where the hell we are. Not a one. We're getting scared again. Too many people staring. Too many strange looks. No brothers. This town must be no good. Back to those tracks double time.

"We just have to keep walking 'cause I know it isn't far. It can't be." Cliff is a confident guy. Walk and walk and walk and walk until about half the day is gone.

"You boys looking for some work?" Wise guy. A chain gang was repairing the roadbed. Working their asses off.

"No man, but we'd like to know how far it is to Memphis."

"You going to Memphis?" He starts laughing.

"Yeah, how far is it?"

"Maybe about 150 miles."

He's got to be bullshitting.

"No wait, Memphis, yeah, that's more like 175 miles. You way up in Tennessee here. We're right next to Kentucky."

That's a lot of walking. And I'm bushed. Falling over these rocks. Thirsty. Big-ass birds giving us the eyeball. And nothing but flat land everywhere. The sun is beating the shit out of us. My ass is about ready to fall off, but we're too scared to stop for any siestas. "Fuck this shit. We're too sick and bushed to the ass to be walking home. Find that highway and let's thumb a ride." Of course the highway wasn't far. We had probably walked parallel to it for several hours.

A truck-driving brother gave us a lift. "You fools really try walking to Memphis? You been out in that sun too long." He wasn't going very far, so he dropped us off at a filling station. We blew my fifty cents on popsicles and cigarettes and then got the bright idea to call home. The operator wouldn't let us reverse the charges and the guy at the station wouldn't let us use his phone. I'm about ready to cry. How the hell did all this start anyway?

Not far from the gas station was a small house and garden— and a sister working in the garden. A lovely sister! Now we're not about to tell her the truth because she'd swear we're both nuts.

"Afternoon, sister. We, uh, had a little wreck up the road and, uh, we wanna go home to Memphis and we'd like to use your phone and reverse the charges. Please."

She talks it over with her husband and they look at us like

we're crazy. But they let us use the phone. Cliff's father answers.

"Cliff, where the hell are you?"

"Look, uh, Dad, we can't explain now, but can you come and get us? Please?"

He explains to his daddy where we are, way up north.

"O.K. You stay there. We'll be right up."

Sighs of relief. This sister asks us if we're hungry. We're starving. Give each other the eyeball. "Yeah, well maybe we'll have a little something to eat."

She says that's fine, but we'll have to be satisfied with leftovers. Leftovers! Sister, we'll eat anything. We went into the kitchen and it was unfuckinbelievable! The table was loaded, half a pig almost, salads, all kinds of goodies. And she called this leftovers. "Help yourself." Finished stuffing our faces, we lit up and thanked the sister. Time to split for the highway. It was getting dark.

We start hoofing it down the center strip of grass on the highway. Hundreds of cars are whipping by us and Cliff thinks everyone is his old man. It's so dark by now, we don't know which side of the road to look on for the car. He may have passed us and be on his way back to Memphis. I've had it by now. So I sack out on the grass. Cliff really has faith in his old man.

"No man, get up. My old man is coming. I know it." We waited and waited. Cliff watching every car for his daddy.

"That looks like it. That's it, man."

Zhoom.

"Cliff, why don't you sit down, man."

"No, no. This is it."

Zhoom.

"Fuck it. Sit down."

A few more cars pass. A few hundred more cars pass. His old man was a chauffeur, so we didn't know whether to look out for his own car or if he'd be driving one of his boss's cars.

A car goes zooming past and out of it comes this scream, "Cliff, Cliiiiff."

Cliff lets out a loud whistle. His old man hits the brakes. Cliff is jumping up and down and I'm stunned with disbelief. He found us in the middle of nowhere! He found us!

His old man stepped out of the car, swearing a blue streak at us. And laughing at the same time. He knew we had learned a lesson.

"Get in, jerks."

We climbed into his station wagon and I went right to sleep. Right off to sleep. All the way to Memphis and home.

THE MOVEMENT AND THE BLOCK

When I was back on the block, at home, TV and the papers were full of the Movement. King was marching here. King was speaking there. But for the brothers on my block, the attitude was just plain "Fuck it." If King comes here to Memphis, there's just going to be trouble and we don't need any. We got our neighborhood to worry about and what happens outside is none of our business. It was like the war in Nam. They are fighting over there. We don't care. They are killing people. We don't give a shit. As long as they don't come in here and start to kill us.

So we never thought much about any movement. We were never really hip to what was going on. That is why we didn't give two shits about it.

We'd watch TV newsreels and see blacks tearing down buildings. Harlem was really hot a few years ago. Then there was Watts. I can remember watching the brothers pulling it down. I thought to myself that these cats must be crazy. What the hell is wrong with them?

There were a few cats in the neighborhood who could not stand whites. But their voices were never heard. They were usually the hoods, the hustlers or at least the kids who were always getting into trouble. So when a cat said that he was never slaving for any white man, we would think that he was just another crazy motherfucker out on the hustle. As for the organized movement, nobody gave it a second thought.

Sure we would get angry and scared when we saw this shit going on in Grenada, Mississippi, where they were even beating little school kids with chains. Please, don't let this happen in Memphis. Grenada was only one hundred miles from Memphis. So we were thinking about it.

What kept Memphis cool then was a story by a white journalist who was sent from Memphis to cover the action in Grenada. Well, the white mob jumped on him and busted up his head. Even smashed his camera. When he returned to Memphis, he wrote about those Mississippi troopers as if they were dogs. They were too insane and barbarian to even be called human beings. This calmed us down a little in Memphis when we read a white reporter writing these things about other whites. We figured that if they also kick white people's asses in Mississippi, they must be crazier than anybody up here.

The TV news programs were almost our sole contact with the Movement. But they showed us only the trouble and the destruction. Never told us anything about why it was happening. So of course our first reaction was always "those crazy motherfuckers." This was in spite of the fact that we realized we were never a real part of America. One remark which I'll never forget describes what we all subconsciously felt. When John Kennedy was mashed, we felt bad. We liked him from what we knew about him on the outside. "I wonder who did it, man. If that cat can make it to Mississippi, he'll be a hero. They'll make him king."

The only place where we really talked politics was at the barber shop, which is the big mouth at home. We were seniors in high school and reading history and government. This gave us something to bullshit about with the old guys. They never listened to us. "No white man ain't gonna let you do nuthin'."

"The white man ain't gonna do shit to stop us because the constitution says so and so and such and such." This would blow their minds. Then sparks would fly.

"Well, boy, I tell you what, if you so bad, you go out there and do it." But the Movement was never a part of us, even though they were killing brothers and sisters in towns all over the country.

The furthest we ever came to showing a little of the old integration spirit was to let white kids play with us on the block. We would always mix up the teams. We knew that if we played against each other according to color, we would all end up fighting. That was integration for us. We had to do it to keep from fighting.

Even in the war, we would try to ignore "the problem." When brothers got together they would rap about their blocks, which one was better. We were always looking the other way. Never mentioned politics. Even in the Nam. While we were there, we would occasionally get some news about the Movement in *Stars and Stripes,* the military newspaper. But it was always about what the hippies were doing. We hated those long-haired assholes. We heard stories about how they would be at the airport when guys returned from the Nam. Calling them murderers, butchers, Nazis. This shit really pissed us off when we read about it out in the goddamn bush. We were hoping that some of these hippies would be around when we returned. Then we could kick some ass.

In general, I never paid much attention to the news we read over there. It was mostly *Stars and Stripes* anyway. When I was in the hospital in Japan, I would only look to see where my unit was and if I knew any guys who were killed or wounded. Never, never a thought about any movement.

Today, it is different. I think about the Movement. I read about what my people are doing and what's happening to them. But I don't know where the hell it is going. It's good sometimes to stand up to the white, say no, kick his ass a bit, burn a little. Then he knows we mean business. It seems to be the only way to get results. But it is also bad when they repress us, kick our asses back. And then we're only burning our own homes anyway. The Panthers, the Black Panthers, look like the only decent group on the scene. They help the other brothers, the brothers on the block. They will work with whites. But unlike Abernathy and his crowd, they will kick ass if attacked. All of which makes sense to me. Because the man has always kicked ass first—and today he is kicking black, white and yellow ass together. So when Carmichael preaches for a split with all other groups, this ain't my game. This does not make any sense to me. While there may be a larger percentage of black babies starving in the States, I know that there are a lot of white babies who are also starving. So we, all those people who are getting asses kicked or going hungry, must band together to attack what is wrong with the American way of life. And if it takes violence, do it. Knock it down and build something better. Unfortunately, there doesn't seem to be any other way now.

But I never thought like this when I was back on the block. The Nam really forced me to think.

HIGH SCHOOL MILITARY TRAINING

I'm sure that a lot of the students and faculty at Lester High School in Memphis were more than a little surprised when they heard that I had split to Sweden. At Lester we had compulsory military training, the National Defense Cadet Corps. I was a gungy motherfucker during those high school military days, always the highest ranked in my classes. Captain McDonald, the CO of Lester's NDCC unit, was very proud of me.

During my first year I was the guidon bearer of my company, A Company. Promoted to color guard commander in my second year. No shit, color guard commander. Probably the only color guard commander in history to march in a Veterans Day parade with the flag upside down!

It was to be a big-time parade. We would be all spit-polished and gleaming. Better looking than the regular military in the parade. We'd be shining our boots and cleaning our gear for weeks beforehand. We were also ordered to paint the school armory for an inspection before the parade. Why that was necessary, I could never figure out.

After all this back-breaking work, we marched—with my flag, the American flag, upside down. It was too windy for me to do anything about it. So each time we passed a cop, he had to salute my upside-down flag. Of course when my ass was chewed out for this, I passed the blame down to the corporal who had rolled the flag.

The military in high school wasn't too bad. The uniforms were smart and the sponsors were good looking. Sponsors were the girls' auxiliary. When someone was commissioned an officer, he received his own sponsor to march around with him. Not bad.

On Wednesdays, we'd get out of class early just to drill. Bullshit. We'd be in that sound-proof armory shooting dice and jiving. I was a master sergeant and supposedly in charge. But it was all jiving until the man came. It was my job to handle the guys who didn't want to cooperate, who didn't want to go along with the program. But more importantly, I knew how to handle the man, Captain McDonald, a retired lifer like all the other instructors.

He was a motherfucker. John Wayne, Ike, Patton, the works. Not at all like the lazy fuckbrain before him, Captain Cox, who just didn't give a shit, only in it for the extra money. McDonald was strictly hard-ass military. He had enough pull with the National Guard to bring them on the campus with a military exhibition, artillery, tanks, the works. At Lester H.S. it was just like the regular military with McDonald as CO.

Every man in the school, in every high school in Memphis for that matter, had to join the NDCC, private and parochial schools excepted. It was a good catch for the military. Put us all in the right frame of mind for what was coming up after graduation. So in sophomore and junior years, we had to put on the uniforms. Senior year was voluntary, but more academic credit was given for the same number of hours if a student enlisted for the last year. I guess it was a good deal if after graduation a student intended to go into the Army, where NDCC graduates were appointed as squad leaders during basic training—which meant no extra duty like KP. Of course the Marine Corps didn't give a fuck. But when I went I at least knew my general orders, could fire a weapon and break it down except for the trigger-housing group.

We had our own firing range at the school, right next to the gym. Three months out of every year, we practiced firing our weapons. So I was in good shape for the Marines. I could take the discipline and I knew my weapon. That's right, I had my own weapon given to me in high school—an M1 fitted to fire .22-caliber rounds.

Strangely enough, we never received much political training.

It was strictly how to be a soldier. Only once did the rifle instructor make any reference to what was going on.

"You should all take great pride in learning how to fire this weapon. It is for your own good, because as a lot of you know, you'll be going to Vietnam next year. So learn while you can."

The real service, the military after high school, was still a big joke to us. We would only jive about it, never giving it a serious thought. People are dying in Vietnam? Not our problem. I did think about it once when a guy who had graduated with the class before me, was shipped back dead from the Nam. A few of us were pallbearers at his funeral. Then, for the first time, I thought about it really being a war. But it still didn't make much of a dent.

I'd read in the newspaper that fifteen guys caught it in the Nam today. And the next day read about fifteen guys who were killed in car accidents in the States. So what's the difference? Get killed in the Nam or get killed at home, same chances. Maybe twenty per cent of the guys worried about the draft, about Sam grabbing us after school. We'd jive about meeting each other over in the Nam. But no one took it seriously.

The year after graduation, almost half my class were in a college of some sort. The rest were in the Army and the Air Force except for two of us. We joined the Marines.

BE A MARINE!

"Sam's gonna get you, babe!"

Me? Shit. What does Sam want with me. A nobody. Just a poor-ass black on the block. Sam doesn't even know I'm alive. The draft? No, that shit just can't happen to me. If they want to fight, let 'em fight. They don't need me.

Dumb motherfucker. That was me when I graduated from high school in June, 1966. Student deferment? I wasn't even sure what it meant. The draft. So what? That was my attitude. A few guys worried about it. Slick dicks who thought they could hustle and bullshit their way out of the Army. They were dumb enough to think that by changing the numbers on their draft cards to 4F, they could slip through Sam's greedy hands. Fat fucking chance—like the local draft board doesn't keep its own files on everybody and his grandfather. Maybe this helped some cats get jobs for a while, because the man would never hire anybody who was classified 1A. But it certainly never kept any cat out of the Army.

Of course my turn did come. "Report for your preinduction physical examination at Kennedy Veterans Hospital." Well, how about that shit . . . maybe, just maybe, Sam has me this time . . . no, impossible. He'll see that I have bad lungs and send me home. No sweat.

Bend over, boy. Spread those cheeks. Cough. Jump up and down. Take an I.Q. test. Congratulations, son! You are fit enough in mind and body to serve in the Armed Forces of the United States of America! Me. Little ol' nobody me. Zapped.

Fuck it. If the man says I have to go, I go. What else am I going to do? Now the problem is where to go . . . who gets my black ass for a few years. If the draft gets me, it's two years in the Army, in the infantry. No class. And guaranteed combat

duty in the Nam. I was an NDCC graduate. A big fucking military deal. None of that diddly Army infantry shit for a gung-ho,
red-blooded American boy like me. Enlistment means an extra
year of active service, but it's also supposed to mean better
duty.

No no no no . . . before I even got through the door, the
Navy recruiter was shaking his head.

"Can't use you. Save your time and try elsewhere. We have a
waiting list of at least three hundred from your district."

White hats. White uniforms. White gloves. White faces. Funny
thing about the Navy, but they don't seem to have many brothers
out there defending freedom on the seven seas.

Air Force. Lots of blacks in the Air Force. Four years active
duty. Nope, too many years. No one left to visit except the U. S.
Marine Corps. They beat me to it. A Marine recruiter came
right up to my front door! A white dude, no less. We commenced
to rapping for a few hours about the joys of being a Marine.
The dude was loaded with pictures taken all over the world of
Marines in dress blues with broads on their arms. Party! Party!
Party! We get you in tip-top physical conditioning for partying
your way around the world. Not only that, but you can take
your sweet-ass time coming into the Marines. One hundred and
twenty days of free time before you go off to the fun and games
of Marine boot camp. That did it. He convinced me with that
last pitch about free time. I could spend Christmas at home
with my family before going into the military. And then if I
honorably completed my three years in the Corps, they'd help
me buy a house when I got out. My own home! Of course the
slippery-tongued bastard forgot to mention that any veteran
from any of the services can get the same deal.

But what the hell, if I have to go into the military, it might
as well be the *real* military. No cheap imitations for me. Go the
gung-ho way. Be a Marine!

"Raise your right hand and repeat after me."

I did. And became the property of the USMC. On February
5, 1967, I packed my little rag bag, kissed my mother good-bye

and hopped the bus for Kennedy Veterans Hospital. About two hundred dudes were hanging around there that morning. Waiting to be shipped all over the country for the beginning of their slaving for Sam.

"All right, I want all my Army men to stand up and move out."

About half the room was emptied.

"Where's my Navy boys? On your feet."

Fifty more dudes shuffle out to the buses.

"O.K., flyboys, move your asses."

Now there were six of us left in the room. Five blacks and one white. All scared shitless. All of us owned—arms, legs, body and balls—by the U. S. Marine Corps. Lucky bastards.

BOOT CAMP

Parris Island.

About the biggest shock in my young-ass life came on the day I rode that bus into boot camp. We're bullshitting, jiving each other. No sweat coming from anybody. The bus stopped in front of a long barracks. They must pick the ugliest DI in the camp to greet the boots when they pull in. Anyway, there he was—Smokey Bear hat and all—on that day I arrived at Parris Island. The ugliest, meanest, fattest DI in the USMC.

"Awright, turds, I want to see nothing but elbows and asses getting off this bus. All cigarettes out."

Now this guy ain't bullshitting. Boosh. We're off that bus and into those barracks. Falling all over each other. Nothing but elbows and asses cramming into those barracks, just like the man said. No more jiving. We know we're in a world of shit now.

The barracks were full of DIs, all of them wearing thick, black belts. None of them looking like they'd even give you the sweat off their asses if you were dying of thirst.

"Now listen up when I'm talking to you assholes. Empty your pockets. Everything out on the tables."

Wallets first. They went through them as if we had just been arrested for picking somebody's pockets. All pictures out. Money out.

"Take off all rings, bracelets, earrings and any other shit you may be wearing, girls."

Jewelry, watches, keys, knives. You name it, we had it and they took it. Screw pictures. Your girl's snapshot. Everything. Into the shitcan, baby.

This first day of boot camp forced us into a new world. The military. Do what you're told and do it fast. Never any questions.

Up to now, we had been used to doing what we wanted to do, when we wanted to do it.

"Sir, may I go to the bathroom?" Ramrod up his ass. Chin in his Adam's apple. This cat can hardly whisper it.

"Whad'ya mean by 'bathroom,' cunt? What the hell is a 'bathroom'? We have no 'bathrooms' in the military."

"But sir, I'm about to do it on myself."

"What you gotta do, turd?"

"Piss, sir."

Two inches from the boot's eyeballs, his new daddy screams, "Tie it in a knot, son. Tie it in a knot!"

At this point we all feel like taking a piss, but we can't even cross our legs to hold it in.

Still on the receiving line, we're a mixed lot. Everyone is in civvies. Nobody looks like anybody else. But these DIs are whacking guys on the side of the head, really kicking ass. Move, turd. Get in line, turd. Shut up, turd. At least we all had received the same name.

Then I spot him. A black face. A brother. A DI who is one of us walks up to our group. We are his platoon. Ooowee, baby. I got it made now. No sweat from here on in. A brother as my DI. He walks up to another black cat in our platoon, our new family.

"You. C'mere. I don't like your face. Your hair. Your clothes. In short, you make me sick."

Boosh. Uunnhh! Right in the gut. This is brother to brother! What kind of shit is this? It ain't going to be no big happy family. Black or no black.

The purpose of boot camp is to turn the boot into a machine. And they start right from the get-go.

"What is your name, turd?"

"Private Joe Blow, sir."

"No, turd. It ain't Joe Blow no more. From now on your name is Two-four-six." That was our platoon number, 2-4-6. We had the same name and supposedly the same color.

"I wanna get one thing straight with you turds. I ain't got no black Marines and I ain't got no white Marines. There ain't but one color here and that's green. Marine green. You understand that, turds?"

I didn't know quite how to take that. But it seemed a cool idea to me at the time. I hear that things have changed in the Marines now. That green color can wear off pretty fast sometimes. It even faded a bit in boot camp.

We had an assistant DI, Sergeant Mitchell, who had been busted a few times. Occasionally he would jump in a brother's shit and kick his ass around the barracks. Then go back to his desk and announce, "You didn't know I was prejudiced, did you? Well, I am, against all my black Marines."

And we just had to stand there and take it. Rigid. This was nothing unusual from Sergeant Mitchell. Once he did surprise me—or at least confuse me. We had all qualified on the rifle range that day. We were the best shots in our battalion. This really pleased him. He was so proud of us, he went off, got drunk and came back to the barracks after lights out. DIs are never allowed to get familiar with their men. But he was drunk and began to rap with us. He started to talk about our senior DI, Sergeant Page, a black.

"I'm proud of this man. Of what he has done. A good wife. A great Marine. He's one colored who has made a success of himself." Mitchell carried on like this for about half an hour.

At first I was pleased. He was praising a black man. But later, in my rack, when I had time to think about it, I was pissed. He had only showed what a bigot he really was. Like it was some big deal for a black man to have a good wife and be a good Marine.

My senior DI certainly was not all that bad in my eyes. As a matter of fact, I really grew to like him. If he didn't crack my head at least once a day, I felt neglected. If he didn't kick my ass or punch me in the stomach at least once a day—well, shit, my DI doesn't love me anymore! What did I do wrong?

Once he actually did hurt me. He was chewing out the unks

back in the barracks at night. Unks are the guys who haven't qualified on the rifle range that day. He was really jumping in their shit. Fire below 191 and a DI gets pissed.

"This is what happens to unks when they don't know how to fire their weapons. When Marines miss their targets, they look like this."

All the unks around the DI's desk were bug-eyed, looking at color pictures of Charlies with their guts hanging out. Their legs, arms, heads blown off. Like all the DIs, he had been to the Nam. And like all lifers, he brought back these souvenir snapshots.

I had fired over 191 that day. Qualified. So I'm stretched out in my rack, resting my ass while the DI is delivering his lecture to the unks.

"Listen up, girls. Starboard side, get in the showers." My side. Grab my little diddy bag and head up to the shower. But as I pass the DI's desk—being a very nosy kind of guy, I sort of glance over there to see what they're all looking at.

"You. You an unk?"

"No sir."

"You. How come you're standin' up here lookin' at these pictures with the . . ."

Boooosh!

Right in my midsection.

"Stand at attention when I talk to you, turd. You're almost a Marine. Did that hurt you?"

"No sir." Gasping for air.

"Oh, you mean to tell me that I'm a Marine and I can't hurt you?"

"I dunno, sir."

He's prancing around me now. Eyeing me up and down. It's coming. From somewhere. Soon. But I ain't moving a cunt's hair.

Boooosh!

"Did that hurt?"

"No sir." It squeaks out from my throat. I'm trying to get

some air down and the words out at the same time. But nothing is working right. I can't even stand up straight.

"I didn't hear you, turd."

Boooosh!

Down. Down on my knees. But it's still "No sir. It don't hurt."

"You callin' me a pussy, turd?"

Boooosh!

His spit-polished black boot right up my ass. It only took a few more shots like this.

"Oh, yes sir, yes sir. It hurts, sir. It hurts all right."

"It hurts? You can't be a Marine if you hurt so easy. I gotta punch you again. Toughen you up a little. Right, turd?"

Boooosh!

Why must my DI love me so much?

"Awright, girls, lights out. In your racks. And if I hear one spring squeak, we gonna watch some television."

One spring squeak? These racks are nothing but a mess of wires and springs with a two-inch mattress thrown over them. How the hell can anybody get in a rack and not make noise?

Squeeeeak!

Seventy-eight guys getting in their racks. Holding their breaths. Trying to tiptoe their asses in gently.

Squeeeeak!

The barracks was full of nothing but rack squeaks. No breathing. Just squeaks. That means *the TV*. Oh no, please no. Anything but *the TV*. Please don't force us to watch television.

"Whitmore, I heard your rack squeak."

Shit. What the hell did he expect. But why me again? There were seventy-seven other cats squeaking away. I've had enough love for one night.

"Girls, we are all going to watch TV now. You can thank sister Whitmore here for doing you the big favor. Out of those fuckin' racks and hit the floor in position."

The front-leaning-rest position. Like we were going to do push-ups.

"No, girls, no. On your elbows. Hands under your chins, girls.

Now we gonna watch television. I like this program. Don't you, girls?"

"Yes sir." Seventy-eight pissed-off idiots screaming.

There ain't no TV program. There's nothing but the jackass across the aisle to look at. And he's doing the same thing I'm doing. Leaning-rest position, elbows on the floor, hands under my chin. It's an endurance contest to see whether my back breaks before my elbows crack. Watching TV.

"Awright, girls, change the station. I don't like this program."

Seventy-eight *uuunnghhs* as we shift our bodies onto our left elbows and "change the station" with our outstretched right hands.

"No, girls, no. You never touch my TV set with your right hand. The other hand, girls."

Over onto the right elbow. Change the station. Stare at the cat in front of me. Or the DI's black boots.

We watched TV for about an hour that night. Bedtime recreation.

Fear is what pushed me through boot camp. Fear of harassment and the beatings from our DIs. A punch or two was always expected. But being beaten up or shit on in front of a whole platoon was too much for any man to take. When it came, there was nothing else to do but take it. The DI would often try to push one of us into squaring off on him.

"Your mother is a whore. I know. I fucked her. She knows how to throw some hump on my dick. You know that, turd?"

Now if any fool said that back on the block, he'd be looking at a switchblade before he could finish. The DI knows this. So he keeps it up, just hoping for an excuse to kick that boot's ass bloody. Street stuff just wouldn't work in boot camp.

My senior DI was a karate expert. On the second day of boot camp training, he got some street punk's goat. Next thing we saw was that punk getting kicked from one end of the barracks to the other.

Fear—piss-in-the-pants fear of the same thing happening to me. That's what kept me going through boot camp. Sure my

DI would dump some shit on me occasionally, but I'd never answer back. My jaws would tighten, but I'd never move an inch.

But it wasn't always fear. Sometimes it was God. God also helped me. Fear from Monday to Saturday. And God on Sunday.

All through the military, the image of God was always with us. At Parris Island and in the Nam, there were Marine Corps chaplains. On Sundays in boot camp, we were forced to go to church whether we liked to or not. I became closer to God during this period than I had been back on the block. The shit we were forced through during the week occupied my mind completely then.

But on Sundays we were left alone. There were no DIs in church—only the chaplain. No DI standing nearby to scare the shit out of me. Knowing that if I even looked out of the corner of my eye, he would come up and punch me in the gut or whack me alongside the head. Church was the only place where I could relax in boot camp. There I could begin to feel a bit like a human being. But only a bit. Even the chaplains would hand us shit about how good Marine Corps training was for us. And how necessary God felt it was for us to do what we had to do when we left boot camp and went to the Nam.

After several weeks of this constant fear plus all the usual ball-breaking training everybody's heard about—and the chaplains telling us how good it all was—we actually started to like it in some weird kind of way. We really wanted to be Marines. But they weren't about to give us that privilege until we had earned it by taking all the shit they had to give.

Every other day, we'd be turning our caps and shirts inside out to hide the Marine Corps emblem. For some stupid reason the DI would feel that we weren't worthy of it that day. Still too pussy to wear the emblem of the USMC. After putting up with all their other shit for weeks and never saying a word, this sort of punishment would really get to us. We were disgraced.

The DIs were so incredibly proud to be Marines. We were envious. We wanted to share some of that pride. To get just a little recognition for making it through this world of shit. After a while, we'd do almost anything for it.

The DIs were always trying to turn us against each other. Each platoon was supposed to hate every other platoon. The DIs would place us in competition with each other no matter what it was about. If someone didn't belong—to your platoon, to the Marines, to your country—he had to be hated on principle.

Once some dude walked through our formation outside the mess hall.

"Get your ass over here, turd. What platoon you in?"

"Two-four-seven, sir."

"Two-four what, turd?"

"Seven, sir."

"This is two-four-six, turd. *My* platoon. You candy asses gonna let this turd from two-four-seven just walk through your formation?"

No sir, no sir. We're tigers. We're Marines. We kill. Two-four-seven? Kick his ass, Jack, kick his ass. And we did, up and down the line.

After chow the DI from 2-4-7 came over to our DI and started in with the my-men-are-better-than-your-men routine. Loud enough for all of us to hear it, of course. But he was a DI and we were not about to kick his ass, as much as we might like to.

"You gonna let him talk about you like that?"

No sir, no sir. Right face and we're off. Our whole platoon marching right into 2-4-7's formation. It was like a big kick-ass on the block. When we entered the USMC, we were turds, cunts, dickheads, girls, pussies, assholes and other assorted forms of non-Marine lower animal life. But now we were at last becoming what they wanted us to be—big, bad Marines. Just doing what we were trained to do. No questions asked. Just do it. Press the button and the machine kicks an ass. The DIs were very pleased with our progress that night.

But if a guy was the type who wouldn't get with the program, the DIs could really bring beaucoup smoke on his ass. Then he'd cooperate with the program. It was like this every day and every night straight through boot camp.

For those three months right up to graduation day, we were never addressed as Marines—everything else but Marines. Each evening before falling into the barracks, we had a platoon formation. At this time we would count off and the platoon leader would report, "Seventy-eight hogs, all present and accounted for, sir." At the end of every single day of this ballbreaking training, after taking all their harassment without a peep of complaint or back talk, we were still not Marines. Just hogs. Had to dump that last ounce of shit on us before we climbed into our racks.

But on graduation day, it was different.

"Seventy-eight hogs, all present and accounted for, sir."

"What did you say, Marine? I see seventy-eight Marines in front of me. I have no hogs in my platoon."

We made it! I could feel that pride actually rushing up my legs, up my back and around my head. I was there! *Wow!* Really a part of that Marine Corps tradition and history which had been drilled into our heads during each and every day of training. The way they taught it, America would have been lost 150 years ago if the U. S. Marines hadn't been there to save it. And now I was a Marine! I belonged to America and the United States Marine Corps. Watch out, America, Whit gonna save your ass!

With all my heart and soul, I honestly believed this shit when I graduated from boot camp at Parris Island.

WELCOME TO THE REPUBLIC
OF SOUTH VIETNAM

Boot camp. Advanced infantry training at Camp Pendleton, California. Vietnam. From boot to grunt in four months. No time to think. No time to worry. Strap on our combat gear in California, walk onto a plane and that's it. It's all over. Or it's just beginning.

Our flight to the Nam was on a commercial airliner. Lots of Oriental stewardesses to make us comfortable. Get us used to the Oriental touch. Half the guys on the plane were Air Force dudes who were loving every minute of it.

"Hey man, I'll bet hers goes from left to right, instead of front to back."

"Yeah, it's slanty, like her eyes."

They could jive because they weren't headed for combat. We grunts didn't say much. This might be our last airplane ride. Charlie is sitting in those jungles right now. Just waiting to shoot our balls off. No grunt on that plane was jiving. We were too fucking scared.

After a stopover in Okinawa, the plane was headed for the crotch.

"Please fasten your seat belts and turn off all lights."

No lights. That means Charlie may be waiting for us right down there on the runway. Can't Sam protect his own goddamn airport?

"Look at that shit. They're fighting down there!"

The flyboys were all eyes. Flares and tracer rounds were popping all over the ground. Couldn't see a thing but these red bursts. I was so scared shitless, that one peek out the window was enough sight-seeing for me. But the flyboys got a big kick out of it.

Whooooosh!

"Christ! We been hit or what?"

The plane made an almost right-angle turn—down. No circling into this airport. Sam has about ten safe square feet down there and we're landing right on it. Dangling from our seat belts all the way down.

"Gentlemen, welcome to the Republic of South Vietnam."

Yeah, knock yourselves out. Have a ball. A stewardess had the goddamn nerve to give us this little speech.

Heat. A sticky wall of heat smacked us right in the face as we stepped off the plane. Jungles. Wartime, baby. We're really here. It was a little hard to believe.

"Air Force over there. Marines this way."

The flyboys get brand-new air-conditioned barracks. We get some wooden shacks and tents. Sack out wherever we can fall. No orders until morning. And no rifle. That worried me. But there was nothing to do about it. Just sack out on some sandbags and pray that Charlie doesn't pop in for a visit.

The sky was full of fire. Flares and firing dragons. I had never seen a dragon before. It's a helicopter loaded down with cannons and machine guns. They call it a dragon because it looks like it's always spitting fire. Every fourth round is a tracer round. But these guns fire so fast that only red lines of fire can be seen coming out of about ten different holes in it. Sweet dreams!

In the morning, the warriors moved in. The grunts back from the bush. Beat to the ass. Muddy. Unshaven. Some a little bloody and all of them armed to the teeth. Ammo belts thrown around their shoulders. They looked like a gang of Mexican bandits. Yeah, this is the real thing all right. War.

After a day of the usual hurry-up-and-wait bullshit confusion, I got my orders.

"You'll be in First Division."

"Where's that?"

"Around Danang somewhere. About thirty miles away."

"How do I get there?"

"That's your problem."

My problem? Who the fuck is running this war? Sam flies me halfway around the world on a commercial jet and when I get there I have to hitch to some place thirty miles away. Where the hell is Danang? I got lost on leave in San Francisco two weeks ago and now I have to find my own way to a spot in the middle of a jungle in a strange country where I can't speak the language or even read the road signs. And there's a fucking war going on!

"If you dudes want a ride, you better come with me 'cause there ain't no other way to get where you're going."

A mail truck. We hitched a ride to First Marine Division, First Battalion headquarters, on an unarmed mail truck. It felt more like running away from home than going to war. Except for the faces of the people in the villages along the road. They were all Oriental and nobody smiled.

"Chop-chop. You give chop-chop?"

Only the kids talked to us, when they were begging for food. I'd never seen kids beg for food before. And I had never seen a Vietnamese. My first look at the people I'd be fighting against.

"Welcome to Bravo Company. Throw your shit in a hootch."

Home for thirteen months. Shacks in a jungle. Warm beer for the grunts. Cold beer for the officers. And guns for everybody.

The battalion commander gave the newcomers a few indoctrination speeches.

"While you are in Vietnam, there will be no liberty."

No shit. I didn't really expect to be partying on weekends out in the bush.

"After six months, you get a one-week rest and recreation vacation. R and R."

Sounds nice. If I last that long. Blahsie, blahsie. He yapped away while most of the guys slept. Never said a word about why we were there. Or what we were supposed to do—other than fight. He did say to be nice to the Vietnamese civilians. Didn't even call them gooks. He actually grooved on the Vietnamese people.

"But stay the hell away from their girls, 'cause they all got the clap."

MY SQUAD

In the Nam we blacks pretty much kept to ourselves, no matter how close we were to our squads. The real bullshitting was always done with other blacks. Jiving about our blocks. Sometimes gambling a little. But in combat the squad was the more important group. No matter what kinds of guys and colors were in the squad, it had to run smoothly if we were to stay alive. Of course we would jive each other about our backgrounds. We were still typical Americans.

This Polish cat and a brother from New York would always be jiving like that. Dumb nigger. Dirty polack. My grandfather used to own your grandfather and whip his ass every day. Shit like that. But just jiving. We even had a Mexican, Durand. We called him the wetback and he'd tell us how his boys kicked our asses at the Alamo. This kind of jiving went on all the time. It never got out of hand. Almost never.

One guy in my squad, Sully the Irishman, was very selfish. He'd get stuff from home and keep it all to himself. We had a little kitchen in the corner of our tent where we would pool all our goodies and eat together. But Sully would sit by himself, stuffing his face. And looking in his mirror. A real Gable. We'd sit around and sing together after chow. He'd be looking in his mirror. So we jumped in his shit whenever we could.

Out on Operation Medina, Charlie had us pinned down and we were dug in. Sully was radioman. Durand was squad leader. They hated each other, but they had to be together. Here we were in the middle of a battle. Durand was short, only a few days left in the Nam. So he was jumpy. Anything happened and he was on the ground fast. Sully became pissed. "Wetback motherfuckin' coward," and took off. Durand went after him. Tracers are flying over our heads and these two are swinging it out. The Mexican and the Puerto Ricans were hotheaded cats. Always ready to fight.

While I was in the Nam, a story appeared in *Stars and Stripes* about Dean Rusk's daughter marrying a Negro. That gave me a bit of the ass and I started to mock it. Sully piped up with his opinion that such a marriage was wrong. He was not jiving this time.

"Sully, it's their own business what they want to do." I was pissed.

Finally it came to the day when Sully and I almost drew on each other. We were way up north not too far from the DMZ. Charlie was everywhere. The monsoon season was ending. The day's rain had just stopped. We were hanging our clothes out to dry. From nowhere, for no reason, he started in with "I remember a name they used to call you a long time ago."

"Say it, motherfucker, just say it!" And I lowered my hand to my .45. I was ready to draw.

He had his .16 and went for it. Right on the trigger. We just stood there, staring at each other for about thirty seconds. If he had raised that .16, I damn sure was going to pull my .45, which was always half-cocked anyway. Not for bullshitting with the guys, but for Charlie. Loaded with a round always in the chamber. If he had raised that .16, one of us would be dead today. Sometimes it was that bad among us.

Otherwise we were a close squad. Even when it was really jumping back in the States, we would only jive each other about it. Especially when that priest was raising hell in Milwaukee. We had one cat from that town. We would fuck with him about his town catching hell.

"When you get home, you gonna have to keep up this Nam shit. You'll be running a listening post just to go to the grocery store."

It was strange that we never jived like this when I first came to the squad. We had a black squad leader then, a real bull jive corporal. He was hit in an ambush a few weeks after I joined the squad. His third heart in the Nam. According to regulations, they had to send him home after three Purple Hearts. The squad changed after that.

We were a groovy squad, really tight when it came to combat. Rarely any bullshit jive then. Just fighting. And stealing. What we couldn't get from company supply, we stole from other squads, other companies. It didn't matter to us. We were very tight when it came to fighting and stealing. Of course if we couldn't steal what we needed, we'd just sell what we didn't want to the Vietnamese and buy back from them what we needed. They always had what we needed. Charlie's cousins always had everything.

GETTING BY IN THE NAM

One of the first lessons we learned in the Nam was to live with a constant fear of booby traps. They scared the shit out of us because there was never any telling where they'd pop up. But in spite of this fear, there were many guys who'd say that if they had to go, they wanted to step on a booby trap. With a booby trap, it was all over in a flash. *Brooosh,* and you're gone, Jack. There ain't no more of you around in one piece. The idea never appealed to me. I could never really relax in the Nam even when I wasn't in combat. There was always the feeling that death was wired to the next bush or lying in the bottom of the next Coke bottle.

Then I ran into Sam's own shit, Bouncin' Betties.

We were out on patrol once with ARVNs. They had stopped for a rest on a hillside. Like typical ARVNs, they just sat there grinning at us. Impatiently we pushed on. Right on into a mine-field which these asshole ARVNs had laid but didn't tell us a goddamn thing about. These particular mines were Bouncin' Betties. When someone steps on a Betty, it bounces up to stomach level, explodes and cuts a person in half. These are the kind that Sam uses. Charlie doesn't have any Betties.

A patrol with ARVNs was usually just diddley-bopping along through the jungle, my mind back on the block ten thousand miles away. ARVNs were not too keen on combat. So if they thought that there would be some shooting, they'd be gone. With ARVNs along, we loosened up, just figuring that we wouldn't run into any fire. Sure, there could always be booby traps. But we never expected these Betties.

A dude up front stepped on one. That's it. Nobody moves. I ain't going nowhere. The guy in back of me urges me to move on. But he is standing stone still. No, Jack, Whit ain't moving. Whit ain't going nowhere for nobody. Just looking down and all around for booby traps and Betties. Bam. Another one goes off up front. Never will I move from this spot.

The man, the lieutenant, tried to keep us all cool and calm. "Just walk out backwards in your tracks, men. Lightly, very lightly."

Boom. There goes another Betty. Somebody else is blown in two.

"I don't know about you dudes up there or you dudes back here, but Whit is stayin' right where he is and don't nobody come near me because I don't want your blood and shit fallin' all over me."

Then the radioman, clumsy as a cow with all that gear on his back, tried to make his way over to the lieutenant. The man wanted to call back to the command post. Boom. Another Betty. The radioman was gone immediately. The lieutenant just lay there with his blood running everywhere and both his legs off. While he was dying, he grabbed the radio almost as if nothing had happened to him. Called back to the CP.

"This is Bravo, second platoon. We're trapped in a minefield. I've been hurt. Several dead. We need some help immediately." And then he was gone. The man just died on the radio.

Nobody would move now. Except for two dudes whose best buddy had been hit. They had been real tight with this cat. The dudes just brass-balled walked over to him, picked him up all bloody and carried him to a spot which they thought was out of the minefield. No can do. They set him down right on a mine. All three of them gone.

By this time we had dudes lying around like dead flies all over the place. We had to get out of that shit immediately. But nobody moved. Nobody except this corpsman, a brother, who just stuck that medical bag on his back and went from wounded man to wounded man. Never looking down, just walking up to each one and giving them a shot of morphine. I admired his courage. But Whit was keeping still. Not moving a muscle.

Finally the skipper, Captain Baker, came to rescue us.

"Listen up now. I want all you men to keep a cool head and a tight asshole. You'll get out of this mess if you just turn slowly and walk out through your tracks."

Through your tracks? A few dudes just had their balls blown off walking in their own tracks! But the man kept it up. "Let's move out, men." Nope, not me. Whit ain't moving. Everybody must have been thinking the same, because nobody in that minefield moved.

At this point, the skipper got pissed and said he was coming in to get us. And he did just that. Straight through that minefield and right up to each and every guy. We all followed him except three stubborn dudes who would not have budged if LBJ himself came and told them to haul their asses out. Finally a chopper had to be called to lift those dudes out of that minefield.

After a few months of experiences like this happening every day, I was a true grunt and ready for a patrol of my own. With combat experience comes leadership. Or so they said. I still didn't see myself as any John Wayne. Not only was this going to be my first patrol, but it would be at night and on listening post. With my usual good luck, this had to be.

"O.K., Hollywood you take the radio." The two of us with three new men who didn't know shit about combat.

Ammo, check—all weapons, check. We move out down this hill. It's my team, but I still have to take point. Have to keep contact with the radioman, keep an eye on the new men. Slowly we're tipping down this hill. We know the place is covered with mines. I don't like it. Hollywood doesn't like it.

It's pitch black. Nothing to see but the outline of these goddamn weird trees. No leaves, just bare arms like they're reaching out, fixing to grab someone. We can hear the cats whining back on the hill. Just like babies crying. No John Waynes here tonight.

I'm still keeping an eye on my men and looking out for that man Charlie. But my balls are in my throat all the time. What happens if someone gets killed? It's my platoon. Who do they blame? Me, Whit. I'm responsible. So of course I'm scared shitless.

Hollywood pokes me. "Look man, I think we oughta stop here. Don't go on down to the point. Just radio back and tell them we're already there."

Well, I'm as scared as he is, but as leader I can't show it. "I'm going, Jack. We're moving."

And we get there all right, everybody in his place. Hollywood sticking to me like white on rice.

This is Whit and I'm a United States Marine and we are at Con Thien. Shit. We got fingers on triggers, necks in shoulders, balls in throats. We're ready. Ready for Charlie. If anything moves, we got it. Dead. But I'm constantly praying for 3 A.M.

When it came, we tiptoed back up to base. We had to tiptoe so as not to scare those jarhead Marines up there into blowing our heads off.

Andy met us. "How'd it go?"

"Cool, man, everything all right. My name Whit. I'm a U. S. Marine."

BRAVO COMPANY

We had just come off a big Operation. Our battalion had suffered almost fifty per cent casualties. My company, Bravo Company, was more fortunate. Below the average with about twenty-five per cent knocked out of action. But that didn't mean we weren't beat to the ass. We'd been in a lot of action in some very rough country. They had trouble flying in ammunition, much less food and beer. So we were starved.

Usually on an operation this big, we would receive C rations for four or five days. All in cans. All on our backs. Impossible. For one thing, there are just too damn many cans. And furthermore, ammo is more important. Ammo had to be packed first. On an operation like this, it would be ammo, not food, which would save a guy's life. I was caught once in an ambush and ran out of ammo. I swore it would never happen again. Pile up on ammo. M.79 ammo. Each round about five inches long. If there was any room left, then pack away some food. Eat up what was left before moving out. This was how I made it.

We were some very hungry grunts coming into the command post. The Seabees had just finished building an airstrip and this CP. Somewhere near Quang Tri. Virgin territory. Not much action here before.

It was about 4 P.M. The Seabees were eating dinner. We grunts had to wait. Wait while these bastards finished eating. That was too much for a bunch of starving, combat-beat-to-the-ass-dragging grunts. Some asses were kicked. And we ate.

After chow, the Captain called Bravo together for some bad news. We would have only one night's sleep, instead of the usual three or so after a big operation, and then move out again. Move out? This had everybody tight-jawed. Even the Captain was pissed off.

The Captain was popular with his men because he always looked out for their interests. Just a few weeks before, when he was still a first lieutenant and a platoon leader, he had refused to take his men out on an ambush. Told a colonel to do it himself. His men were too exhausted. The colonel found another platoon. He wasn't about to jump in the Captain's shit. He was too valuable a leader.

But this time there was nothing the Captain could do for us. Bravo was the only company with enough men left to move out on short notice. The CP had drawn some mortar fire from the surrounding hills. Somebody had to go up there and wipe them out. Then check over a nearby village to make sure that Charlie wasn't holing up in it. This job went to Bravo Company, three platoons and a mortar unit. My company.

The Captain never took any chances with the Viet Cong. He never gave Charlie an even break. The story in the company was that his brother had been killed in the Nam and he had enlisted to get revenge. I don't know how true that was, but the Captain certainly was a guy who hated Vietnamese.

"Men, if we get one sniper round, just one, we gonna level that village. Just level it. We're not taking any more shit."

The pep talk really had us grooving. We're going to see some real fucking action. Kick ol' Charlie's ass. This is how the company felt. If we can't be drinking beer back in the rear, we might as well be kicking some ass.

We moved up this hill to Charlie's mortar position. Nothing. Charlie had split. We checked out the hilltop and moved down the other side towards the village.

Piiing!

Sniper. That does it. Everybody digs in fast and sets up. I'm already dinging away on my .79. The mortar team is all set to go.

Boop.

Booosh!

Nothing. We don't know whether or not we got him. He never fired again. But it was enough for the Captain. He was pissed. He had us up and moving down the hill. Down to the village.

"Well, men, there it is. Level it."

Very calm. No emotion in his voice. He meant it. Just level it. One sniper burst and the Captain was true to his word. Now that it was sitting right in front of us, this was hard for some of the guys to believe.

"Level it."

Now there are a hell of a lot of people in this village.* Men, women and kids. I don't know exactly how many, but there are thirteen hamlets full of them. Plus a lot of livestock.

"Level it."

We had a bunch of real go-getters who didn't have to be ordered again. Eyeballs bulging. Safeties off. These cats were more than ready to go at it. Marching right through this village. No resistance. Not a shot. We didn't even see a weapon all that day. Other than our own, of course.

It happened every time we hit a village. A crowd of people would run into one hootch. The chief's hootch, probably. A mob was trying to squeeze into this one hootch while some of the guys started to burn. They were burning every hootch. If somebody ran out from a burning hootch, the guys would shoot. People started to die immediately. Right at the beginning of the day.

We split up into fire teams and moved around the hamlets and into the fields where the livestock were kept. Nobody was told to do anything specific. Each guy went ahead and did whatever he felt like doing. Burn, shoot or just roam around. Of course a guy couldn't look as though he were just out sightseeing. So the livestock made good targets for anyone who wanted to get away from the village and its dying people. One

---

* Although T.W. uses the term "village," it was probably a *hamlet* consisting of thirteen *subhamlets,* as they are officially classified according to number of inhabitants.

of my sergeants spent the whole day chasing chickens and plugging them.

I headed up towards the herds.

As I'm dinging away at this herd on the hill, our second gun-team sets up an M.60 machine gun on the other side of the field. My .79 rounds explode around the cattle. They stampede right into the fire of the M.60. We killed every single head of cattle and water buffalo. Cut them all down. We had to do something to keep busy. We weren't up for killing unarmed people. But we couldn't seem too good for fighting, better than the other guys in the company.

The first gun team was back at the chief's hootch. Mainly women were inside. The M.60 was set up outside the hootch. Back about ten yards. Aimed right across the front door. A Marine with his M.16 went in and forced these people out of the hootch at gunpoint. Just running them out and into the fire of the .60. I could see the whole scene from my spot on the hill. A complete slaughter. Every single one of those Vietnamese people were cut down. Not one had a chance to escape. That took care of most of the adult inhabitants of the village. The rest of that day was spent burning the hootches, killing anyone who was left and looking for Charlie's supplies. We never found any.

Although the whole scene was disgusting, there was one brother who especially pissed me off. He had rounded up an old monk. Just some old guy. No gun. No back talk. Just some old guy shuffling along in front of this brother who's dinging away at everything in sight. Then all of a sudden, *brraaak*. This monk is everywhere. He didn't have a chance to say or do anything.

This is my company. Bravo.

We went through all thirteen hamlets in the same way. Burn. Kill the adults. Shoot the livestock. As the last hamlet was going up, one of the squad leaders spotted a hootch off to the side. Almost in the bush.

"Captain, we got one hootch left."

"Send a team over and get rid of it."

"Whit, take your team and do a job on that hootch."

Skip, a few other guys and myself. We headed towards the hootch. It's standard operating procedure to lay in a round or two when approaching something like a hootch.

Boop.

No *boosh.* I was too close to detonate a .79 round. It just bounced off the side of the hootch. An M.79 round is a grenade which has to be fired at least 15 meters before it explodes. We were too close to this hootch.

I was about to tell the guys to stand back and fire a few .16 rounds at the grenade to detonate it, when an old Vietnamese woman with a little boy came running out of the hootch and up to me. The other guys started to burn her hootch.

"Take these papers. Take these papers."

I guess that's what she's saying to me in Vietnamese because she has a handful of documents, medals and pins which she's forcing into my hands. I don't know what the hell this old lady is trying to tell me. She's carrying on in Vietnamese and all her papers are in Vietnamese.

"Go away, lady. Just go hide. Take your boy and go hide."

The rest of the company was pulling back to the first hamlet. Mopping up as they went. Wasn't much left. Just some kids. We broke out in a run to catch up with the company. Started to had it up.

Boooosh!

An explosion in back of us. Hit the dirt fast and spin around. It was my .79 round. I had forgotten to detonate it. The kid must have picked it up and started playing with it. He and the old lady were gone. I hate to say what happened to them. Just that they were gone.

For the first time in the Nam, I got sick. Sick to my stomach.

By the end of the day, by the time it started to grow dark, all the adults had been killed. A few at a time. But eventually all of them were dead. All the hootches had been leveled. Burned. All the livestock had been shot. Only the children were still alive. If any of them had been killed, it was accidental. Nobody intended to kill a kid.

Then we hit some resistance. But not from the kids. From a booby trap. We had made it through the day without one casualty. We never drew any fire except for the sniper burst that morning.

As we made our way back through what was left of the village, a brother—a corporal who had trained with me at Camp Pendleton, California—stepped on a booby trap. It tore open his legs. There wasn't much to be done except call for a Medevac chopper.

When a chopper lands, especially at night, a perimeter has to be set up. The wounded brother, myself and a few other guys waiting in the center.

The Captain comes up to the radioman who's with us.

"Get me the last squad. I wanna know what the hell is taking them so long."

"We got all the kids down here, sir. Got 'em all rounded up. Where should we bring them, sir?"

"Bring them? What the hell you talkin' about? You know goddamn well what to do with them. Now."

"Sir?"

"You kill them, Marine. You hear me? You kill them. This is what I want you to do with them. Now."

Silence.

Goddamn! This man ain't bullshitting. This man ain't human! Just like that, kill them. Now Marines are usually freaks about kids. Try to be good to them, avoid hurting them. We're all staring at the Captain. Swearing that he must be crazy. Nobody kills kids intentionally.

"Marine, if you ain't got the balls, bring them up here. Bring them to me. And I'll do it."

It was very quiet now. Nobody in that perimeter said a word. The radio was off.

Brrrraaaakk.

One long burst. And then a few single shots finishing off. It lasted about a minute. M.16s on automatic. Maybe a gun team too, I'm not sure. About a minute. Then it was quiet again. We couldn't see anything from our position. We only heard the firing.

Medevac came and carried out the wounded brother. We spent a very quiet night there and then moved out in the morning. The CP wanted us to look for another mortar emplacement. We found it, but Charlie was gone. An ambush was laid in. Charlie never came back. We returned to the CP that night.

Typical gung-ho Marines, they started to shoot their mouths off. Man, you should have seen us level that vill! Went right through it. Burned the whole fucking thing! The word spread around to the men in the other companies. We were a proud company.

After a day or so, one kid started to get soft. All this shit got next to him. He was going crazy inside. Tearing him up. He spilled everything to the chaplain. Then the shit hit the fan.

The chaplain went straight to the battalion commander. The Captain was relieved of his command. The first platoon, his old platoon, which had been with him through this entire operation, was confined to the compound. The rest of the company was placed under a temporary command and sent out on other Operations.

When we returned, it was all over. Civilian investigators in fatigues had swooped down on the CP and done a job on the first platoon. Odd that they questioned only the Captain's old platoon. We were just as guilty. The rest of us had killed and burned as much as the first platoon. But only the old boys caught the heat.

"Yeah, these assholes came around and asked a lot of questions. But I didn't say nuthin', man. They didn't get nuthin' outta me. I don't know nuthin'. When I get shot at, I shoot back. That's all I know."

Some lifer sergeant must have clued them in on what to say, because they all popped up with the same answers. It was all taken as a big joke.

"I don't know nuthin'. When I get shot at, I shoot back."

The investigators had swarmed all over the place with their clipboards and papers and maps.

"That village was marked as a friendly village. You weren't supposed to touch that village."

O.K. It's supposed to be friendly. They take their notebooks, clipboards, maps and the first platoon. Off to look at what's left of the village. As soon as they came within sight of that village, Charlie opened up with everything. Hit them with all kinds of shit. Of course the first platoon had anticipated this.

"Yeah man, you still think this is a friendly village?"

We had just wiped out everybody we caught in that village. If the Vietnamese here were friendly once, they weren't friendly anymore. Of course Charlie would have to get revenge. These people were pissed.

Now it was the enemy's territory.

I know that first platoon was transferred to another company. Rumor had it that the Captain was thrown out of the military. The rest of us with our new commander, a black, were shipped back up north to Con Thien.

I often think about those kids. Not only the ones who were killed that day, but even the kids who are still alive. What the hell is going to happen to those kids? Their parents are dead. They know nothing but war with guys like us. Guys like the grunts in Bravo Company.

CON THIEN

Con Thien, that godforsaken hill. It was without a doubt one of the most feared combat zones in the Nam. Con Thien meant beaucoup pain to any grunt. Four, five hundred rounds a day. Charlie was always throwing stuff in there. Mortars, rockets, artillery--all kinds of canno coming in on our asses. We were right in Ho Chi Minh's backyard on the DMZ.

On the night of December 14, 1967, we were preparing to move out for a major ambush the next day. I was usually lucky enough to pull the last hour of guard duty. This means a night of uninterrupted sleep before going on. That is if Charlie doesn't come around for an evening visit. My buddy, Moe, was always sitting guard in the hole next to me. This particular night we were out there on the perimeter, just rapping. Broads on the block, school—shit like that. We jived that night, just like every other night. Moe and I were very close raps.

Before daybreak, we were all up, strapping on our ammo and applying carbon to our faces for camouflage. I have to admit that I could never figure out why I had to put black on my face. It looked goddamn silly. But orders are orders, so I just go along with the program. Put black on black and rub it in good.

Sully was the lieutenant's radioman that day. So Hollywood had the squad radio. Both of them were with the lieutenant when he came down to give us our last-minute instructions. A nice guy, but a green glory-hunter, hot to make rank fast.

"No smoking out there. Smoke your last cigarettes now. When we get out there, I want absolute quiet."

We'd been in combat for half a year. But he's talking to us as if we didn't have enough sense to be quiet on patrol. As I said, he was a green-assed lieutenant.

"First squad, first platoon, point."

Who's that? Us. We got to take the point. Everybody is tight-jawed at this. Why us? Why do we always have to put our asses on point?

But we moved out. My buddies were all with me. Cope as point man, a Puerto Rican cat on cover, I'm third with my .79, Andy was behind me, Hollywood behind him, then Perez and the rest of the guys. It was slow- but casual-going. Cope was cautious. He felt what we all felt. Something was going to happen and there was no way to avoid it. Just keep moving through the bush until we hit it. Whatever it is.

At about a thousand meters before the DMZ, there was a huge gray pile of rocks. This was our destination point. When we arrived, we were supposed to direct all the others behind us into position. I took my fire team there, moved in and immediately hooked up our radios. Now there was nothing else to do but wait. Daylight was beginning. So I'm no different from everybody else. I get myself deep down in the bush where the man can't see me and light up. But quietly, always quietly. I had a book with me. Started to read my fuck book. Hid that when the lieutenant came around to check our lines.

"Yes sir, we see anything move and we'll contact you."

So I told everybody to keep their eyeballs peeled while I went back to my fuck book. This was nothing unusual. Hollywood and I once read a fuck book right in the middle of combat. Shit was flying all over the place. We were on top of each other in a bomb crater and he's screaming at me to turn the page. "They're fixin' to do it, man!" Right under all this canno coming in on us and he wants to look at a fuck book. So it was no big thing for me to be reading one on this day at Con Thien.

Once they called me on the radio. "All secure, post three, sir. Don't see nuthin'."

It was six o'clock in the morning and we were secure. We sat that way until about eleven o'clock. Nothing moved. It just stayed quiet in the bush. No life at all.

What we did not know was that Charlie had moved in and was sitting no more than fifteen meters away from us. We were in one line. Charlie was in another directly parallel. So we sat all morning, neither one of us knowing that the other was there.

One of their officers gave them away when he started to check their line. They probably didn't have radios like we had, so he had to creep along from one guy to the next to make sure that nobody was sleeping or bullshitting. Hollywood and Andy were the first to spot him.

"Two enemies spotted, sir, about fifteen meters in front of us. Wearing light ammo."

That took me from my book for a while. I told my men to stay in position and continue to watch towards both the front and the rear. Then two or three rounds went off. *Ping ping ping.* Time to get my head and ass way down. Some of our boys started to return fire. But Charlie was smart, kept his cool and split from sight.

Now our lieutenant comes up, screaming orders, letting everybody in the whole goddamn jungle know who he is and what kind of rank he has. Typical glory-hunter! He wants to move up.

We're up and moving. Nobody knows that there is a whole enemy company out there, just fifteen meters away. The lieutenant assumed that it was only the two or three we spotted. He figured we could knock off two or three with no trouble. Those of us who had been in combat knew better. Up north Charlie never travels in twos and threes; he is there at least in company strength.

"Whit, Whit come over here." The lieutenant wants me. I was the only one of the three .79 men in the platoon who had any combat experience. "Whit, up! Whit, up!"

I grabbed my .79, strapped on my ammo. Look out, Jack, 'cause here I come. I had it up, running to see what the man wants.

"Whit, I want you to lay a couple of rounds in those bushes over there."

Pong, boosh! Pong, boosh! I'm down on my knees, shooting away with the .79 and nothing is happening. Nothing moved.

"That's good, Whit. Now we're gonna move out, men."

Move out? Goddamn, this man is crazy! This young turd has been in Nam a month, a few patrols. Finished boot camp, rushed through officers' training school, all in ten weeks. And now the fool wants us to put our asses right in front of Charlie's guns so he can blow all our balls off. I had just fired a few rounds over there. I didn't see any blood flying around. I didn't see any guns go anywhere. Nothing moved. Nothing was hit. Charlie still has got to be out there.

We just stared at one another, all thinking that this young lieutenant is a complete fuck brains. But orders are orders. So we moved out. The man was on my right. This Italian cat was on my left. The whole platoon is moving out in a straight line, right into this open space. I'm too scared to say anything, but I know that something is going to happen. We tipped out there, slow and quiet. Everybody but this lieutenant. He was still shouting orders. He really pained my heart. I felt sorry for this jerk who was telling the whole jungle that he was an officer. It pained me even more, because I was standing right next to him.

We were no more than five or six meters out into the open when the whole world just turned to shit. Everything opened all at once. AKs, .50 caliber, .30 caliber. Of course the lieutenant was one of the first hit. He had been about a foot in front of me. All I saw was his body flying past. I was already on the way down and turning fast. You don't think too much in combat. It is almost all reflex action. And my reflexes said to get the hell out of there.

I made it back to the bush with this Italian right behind me. The rest of my whole platoon were still out there, pinned down. Those who were not dead could not move, could not even raise their heads to fire their own weapons.

The two of us just lay there behind this rock, just staring at each other, still shocked. Then I heard this voice. It was the first human sound I heard after the gunfire. It was the lieutenant and he was calling for me.

"Whit, Whit? I'm hit, Whit. I'm hit."

Why me? I'll never know. Perhaps it was because I was the last person he saw. He just continued to scream for Whit. I just looked out fast to where he was lying, then glanced back at the Italian. "Cover me. I'm moving out there. I got to go and get the man. He's callin' me. He's callin' Whit."

Now I had been in a lot of combat, so I knew that my .79 was like my arm or leg. But I wasn't thinking then. I just put it down and took off running with my .45 still in its holster. Now I'm moving, Jack. I had it up to the man. Bullets are flying all over the place. But I still ain't thinking. Just running to the man because he is dying. Me get killed? Never entered my mind.

On my way, I ran right by a Charlie. Right by him! And he just watched me. Didn't shoot, didn't move, nothing. He just watched me run by.

The man was lying on his side when I got to him. I hit the ground and turned him over, still screaming, "Whit, I'm hit." As I was moving him, I caught a glimpse of this Vietnamese again. Charlie had his weapon pointed right at me. As I lifted the lieutenant up in my arms, I heard the round go off. The man in my arms jumped, moaned and sagged. He had been hit again. This time in his leg.

What could I do? There was only a .45 in my holster, but the man was hanging in my arms. So I just threw the lieutenant over my shoulders and the two of us had it up back to the bush. Running right beside Charlie again, right in front of him! I could not allow myself to think about him. Just keep running and hope to God that if he shoots, miss. Please, don't hit me.

This man could have made spaghetti out of me. But he just lay there and watched me with the lieutenant pass directly in front of him. "Damn fool. He must be a damn fool" was all that went through my mind. Later I got to thinking that maybe, just maybe, it was the color of my skin that kept me alive. The lieutenant was white. Charlie was yellow. I'm black.

The man had a hole straight through his chest. I could see this when I took off his flak jacket. "You're O.K., sir. You gonna make it." Got to keep his morale up or he will go right into shock and die on me.

"Tell the skipper I'm sorry. Tell him I'm sorry." He kept repeating that because he knew that he had been wrong to lead the platoon out into that open space, no cover, nothing.

I tore off his shirt and put his first-aid patch over the hole in his chest. It was a small hole where the round had entered. Then I rolled him over and put my first-aid patch over the huge hole in his back. There was nothing to put on the hole in his leg.

Bullets were still flying. Rounds were exploding everywhere. All those dudes were out there crying. Mommy, Daddy, Corpsman, God! But nobody knew that they were there. They weren't going to get any help.

I was still on my knees, pulling the man back. He was no featherweight. It took a long time to get him deep into the bush. Two Marines spotted me when I let him down and came over to help. Those rounds were still whizzing by, but they just stood there with a nonchalant "What's wrong, man?"

"Give me your first-aid pack, man, this is the lieutenant and he's hit." I wound that patch around the man's leg and then stood up for a minute. *Crack*. Bullets flying in our direction. Got my head down fast. It was unbelievable. The man on my right was hit. The man on my left was hit. But I was saved again. Not a scratch.

And then there was Sully, running around with the radio on his back. Sully did a fantastic job that day. He'd run around to each of the wounded, at least those wounded he could reach. "Everything all right, babe. You gonna be O.K. Charlie barely scratched you."

He was lying through his teeth, but it kept those dudes from going into shock. In between talking to the wounded, he was calling back to base camp. "Look, man, we're hit real bad. Here are our coordinates. Now get us some help fast."

So artillery started to lob in these big smoke rounds to give us some cover. Sully is still moving through all this. Talking to every guy with a hole in his body.

"Sully, you gotta help me with the lieutenant. I got two other guys who are also hit."

Sully got down on his knees to talk to the lieutenant. I'm still yes-sirring him, but Sully just starts to rap. "The man got you, babe, but he's a shit shot. You gonna be up to kick Charlie's ass tomorrow." Now he had to talk like that because if he started in with "Oh, my God, sir, what the hell they done to you?" the lieutenant would be gone. Right into shock. "We got to get this man out now, Whit, before he dies."

At that point we could hear Hollywood screaming, "Corpsman, Corpsman." We couldn't move. But there was a new corpsman, brand spanking new and scared shit, crawling through the bush.

"Over there, man, over there. Go help Hollywood." He wasn't about to move at first. But Sully made it clear that if he didn't get his ass over there, we would plug him before Charlie could. He moved out with his face about two inches into the ground, he was so scared.

Before he left, he threw us a roll-up stretcher for the lieutenant. We put the man on it. Now we had to get out with him. Sully wanted to get up and make a run for it. I wanted to crawl. We tried to run. Sully grabbed the back, I had the front. We're up and running. One, two, three steps. *Cracks.* Then the stretcher went limp. The weight pulled me back down. Sully had been hit.

"Sully, are you all right?" No answer. He just rolled over and over, laughing all the time. Laughing! He has been hit, but he's laughing. Charlie got him right in the ass and Sully just could not believe it.

"The motherfuckers! They got me. They got me in the ass."

"You O.K.?"

"Yeah, yeah. Just get the lieutenant outta here. How could they hit me? Me? And right in the ass. No, man, no."

I'm back on my knees now, dragging the stretcher. The bullets still steadily flying over our heads. The lieutenant was safe, out of the fire. But Sully was back there. I had to get him. Turn around and back I go, nothing but a .45 in my hand. And it ain't worth shit at that distance.

On the way back, another Negro moved in behind me. "What's up, bro?" This big black cat just crawling along, arm over arm, cool as a clam. "What's up, brother?" M.16 in his arms; he was one of those real go-getters. "C'mon, c'mon, Jack. We're movin'."

When we reached Sully, he was still laughing and trying to speak into the radio phone at the same time. Smoke and mortar were pouring in now. Sully was starting to show the pain all over his face. The muscles in it were tight. His body started to shake. We had to get him back to where the lieutenant was. I lay on my stomach. The other brother was right next to me. Sully was lying on our backs with his arms around our necks. He had just about had it by now. His head was hanging. There was pain all over his face. About halfway out, he raised his head. Looked at me, looked at the other cat.

"Ya know, Whit, I never thought I'd see the day when I would be so glad to see two splibs." Splibs is old Navy slang for Negro. Bullets were still flying all round, but Sully had to give his great brotherhood speech.

"Now ya see, we ain't all bad." This is what the other brother said. I'm taking this cat out of war and he's running off at the mouth like that. And then, "We ain't all bad." What kind of shit is that? But this is combat. All that matters is that we get our asses out fast.

We dragged Sully to a huge B-52 bomb crater. That should have been the end of it. Safe. Out of combat. But I could still hear those guys crying. Momma. Poppa. God! My platoon. My buddies are down there catching shit. They're dying. This got next to me.

"I need some help. Somebody to go in there with me. Gotta get those guys out." Nobody even looks at me. They're looking here, there, everywhere but at me. Fuck you then. I loaded seven rounds into my .45. Took off my .79 ammo jacket. Put my flak jacket back on. Started out again. Over the top of the bomb crater and sliding along the ground like a weasel. Right back into all that shit.

"What's up, brother?" He's still with me. Big shit-eating grin on his face. Crawling along with his M.16. Didn't say a word. Just "What's up, brother?" So we move out, staying low all the time. We practically crawl over another Marine, a white dude, who is headed in the same direction.

"What's up, man?"

"It's my platoon out there. I gotta go in and get them." At about this time I started to scream to Hollywood for some direction.

"Over here."

At that I got up and ran like hell. Why? I'll never know. Just up and like hell through the fire. The man was dinging away at me. But no luck. Sorry, Charlie. I made it in and hit the ground.

No man, it just couldn't be! My face was right on top of these boots. I crawled up over the body, which was lying in tall weeds. Who was he? Was he still alive? When I reached his face, I saw a first-aid patch covering it. Andy, Hollywood and that green corpsman were all nearby. Perez had been shot in the chest. His lung was punctured. He couldn't breathe. Just rolled over and over, his body twitching and jerking all the time. A plastic cover had to be placed over the hole in Perez's chest to keep some air in his lungs. While the corpsman was trying to do this, the other two held Perez down.

So who was this guy underneath me? When I saw the face clearly, I recognized him immediately. It almost broke my heart. It was Moe. I think he had been shot in the head. I laid on him and wanted so badly just to grab him and wake him. Get up, man, get up. We had been rapping and bullshitting all night. He ain't dead! Moe, you got to wake up, man! I reached for the patch.

"No, Whit." Hollywood stopped me. Then I knew for certain that he was dead. He wasn't going to do anything with those broads back on the block. Moe was gone.

"I'm gonna get me some motherfuckers. I'm gonna kill me somebody. Where are the rest of our guys?"

They were six or seven meters in front of us. By now the two Marines who were following me had reached my position. The brother took the radio from Hollywood. Andy just looked at me. "You're crazy, man" was in his eyes. But all he said was "Whit, keep your head down."

I was only half out from behind the rock when Charlie spotted me. He was up in a tree. *Bbbbbrrrr.* Bullets all around my head. Back behind that rock fast. "Throw some smoke, man. Throw the smoke!"

The brother with the radio let loose with a target smoke canister attached to the radio. Out again into the yellow smoke. We reached the others in a hole behind a big rock. The other .79 man was there wounded five times. Two guys were trying to work on him. A .60 machine gun was sitting up in front of the hole. But nobody was firing it. They were all too stunned, just lying there.

"Hey, what's wrong with the gun?"

"Nuthin'."

"So why the hell ain't you shootin' it?" I'm catching all kinds of shit from Charlie while this big gun is just sitting there.

"Andy, throw me your .79. You guys, out of the hole. Get the hell out of here." Started to pull one guy out by his arm. *Whack!* It explodes right in my face. His right arm was hit. Christ, but Charlie is getting closer every time. This guy could still crawl. He got the hell out of that hole fast.

But this Charlie was still popping away at him from his hole on the tree line. He was a good shot, so I wasn't wasting any time aiming my .79. These had to be quick up-and-down shots. *Poop. Boosh!* First round on his right. This gave him a bad case of the ass. *Bbbbrrrr.* He's at it again. *Poop. Boosh!* One more popshot on his left. *Bbbbrrrr.* Charlie is still pissed and shooting. Now it was almost a game between the two of us. Guys may be dying all around us, but we two clowns are playing games.

Next time, I kept my head up a few seconds longer just to get some aim. *Poop. Boosh!* Gun, blood, everything came flying out of Charlie's hole. One of my best shots ever.

The brother had led all the others back. Now it was only me and this white Marine left in the hole with all their weapons. Now we are going to have us a real party, Jack!

The jets had come. Flying around over our heads. We called them and now they're with us. On our side, babe. Charlie's ass is gone. Spotter rounds are dropping all over the place. Red smoke. Enemy. Drop your bombs on this. Charlie knows what red smoke means.

Charlie started to scramble out of his holes. Marvelous! We just fired away. One hundred round belts on the .60. Me with my .79 and a .16. If we killed one, we must have killed twenty-five. Just cutting them down. But Charlie didn't give a shit. It was be killed by us or the bombs. And he stands no chance against the bombs. So he had it up. Out from those holes. We were not missing. We were not missing one swinging dick. Party time. Red smoke right over us? Fuck it. We're on the same side. They can't hit us. We're partying, babe. Oooh, get some, Jack, get some motherfuckers. Kill, kill, kill is all we know. Typical jarhead Marines.

Then the shit hit the fan. A tank. A big-ass tank was moving up from our rear. Firing its main gun. *Brooosh.* Right over our heads. Exploding in front of us. Fool! Doesn't he know we're here? Didn't those clowns tell him that two more men were still out there? "Hey, fool, don't be shootin' at us. We're on your side, babe." But it was no big thing for him. *Brooosh.* His big motherfucking bomb goes off right in front of us.

Now Charlie wants this tank out. It can always chew his ass up bad. He didn't know that it was only there to pick up the wounded, then move out. Mortars. Charlie starts to lob in mortars. We're in a cross fire now, and those jets are starting to circle lower. Mortar round lands right next to us. Another behind us. Charlie has got us zeroed in. Get the fuck out now. The next poop and whistle has got to land on us.

With my .45 out, I start to move back slowly. On my knees, crawling backwards. Thank God, I went slowly. *Pzzzzz. Booosh.* My moving a little faster and it would have been direct.

I'm hit. Oh God, I'm hit. The concussion had picked me up and thrown me back into the rock. My body felt like a rubber band. Everything was loose-dangling. Nothing was still. My vision was gone. Everything was moving around and around, outside and inside me. My body, my mind—it was all like soft rubber.

I was scared to look down at my legs, certain that they were gone. No, they were still there. Soaking wet and all pain. It was not that hot, so I knew that it wasn't sweat all over my legs. My pants had been blown away. What was left was all open and running with blood.

"How bad am I hit, man?"

"Not bad. C'mon, we gotta move."

He was slightly wounded in the back. Some shrapnel caught him. But he could move. My legs were just blood and pain. I could not move. They say that just before you split the scene, you see your life go by in a few seconds. Well, it's no bullshit. Everything in a few seconds. As a kid at home, the block, my schools. All of it was right before my eyes. I was ready to pack it in then, babe. Just pack it in. No matter how much I tried, no movement. My .45 was frozen into my hand. You would have had to cut off my hand to get it. But it wasn't doing me any good then. I was paralyzed.

The tank was backing out, but still firing away from our rear. The jets were circling lower. Charlie was lobbing in his mortars. That goddamn ground never stopped moving. The white Marine was hanging in there. He'd look at each threat in sequence, then back at me. He did this several times. It seemed as though he didn't know which one to react to first.

"Move, man. You got to move now. We gonna be dead soon if you don't move."

Not a muscle. Nothing. I kept trying. I used every bit of strength in me. But still nothing moved. Not one single inch could I move away from that world of shit. It was very hard at first for me to realize that I was about to go. I had almost given in to the idea. I just wanted to sleep. Until I thought about my little girl, who was born after I came to the Nam. My mother was taking care of her. She'd never see her father now. I'll never know her. All this shit started running through my head.

Once more the white Marine looked at me, at the enemy, up at the jets. His hand touched my arm. Creeping along until he reached my shoulder. He grabbed me. On his gut, he started to drag me out. He was wounded. He couldn't stand or even kneel. I couldn't help. He just dragged me through the dirt, back about five or six yards. He turned me over.

I saw them. The worst motherfucking sight I had ever seen in combat. We're praying for help. Like God, I'm dying. Then we look up and all we can see is the point of an F-11 Phantom jet coming directly down on us. These are U.S. jets. I'm supposed to be with you. We're fighting together, man! I'm paralyzed. I can never get away from these fucking bombs!

The white Marine just pushed my body into a hole and lay on top of me. The Phantoms, two of them, rolled in and dropped a few two-hundred-pounders about thirty or forty meters in front of us. Thank God it was not napalm. We would have been fried to death immediately. Phantoms drop four bombs at a time in each pass. Each time one went off, we were lifted off the ground and smashed back down. Over one hundred pieces of shrapnel in me which these concussions are driving deeper. The pain was ripping me apart. Nothing but pain each time one of those motherfucking bombs went off.

"Hold on, babe. You gonna be all right." He's still jiving with me. Keeping me out of shock. Without his encouragement I surely would have gone in shock and died. If this cat were ever to run for President, I'd vote for him. He could be a racist, but I'd still vote for him. That's how grateful I am to him.

"Look, man, you're a Marine. We gotta get more Charlies. You ain't allowed to die out here."

"Yeah sure, man."

The planes were gone now. It was quiet. We're still down in that hole.

"Hey, man, you got a cigarette?" There I am dying and this dude wants a fucking cigarette.

"No, man," I whispered.

"What kind of a fuckin' Marine are you, man, walkin' around with no smokes?"

This man might have been nuts, but he kept my morale up. Kept me alive. Kept me from thinking about dying.

FIELD HOSPITAL

My first hospital was a field hospital. They had brought me there with some of the dead on a Medevac chopper. It is depressing to see the way they throw the dead around in the Nam. But luckily I was only half-dead.

They ran me in and onto a table. The doctors swooped in and started to cut off what little clothing was left. Even my boots were cut off with these sharp scissors. Took those boots right off. This gave me the ass because I had always wanted to have those boots bronzed.

It was cold lying on that table. I couldn't stop shivering. Some dude gave me a cigarette. I could see the other guys in my outfit getting patched up. Those who were still alive.

Just five tables away from me was a face I could never forget. I nearly shit when I saw him—Sergeant Abernathy, my DI from boot camp. He had been shot up about four or five times while leading Alpha Company in to help us. He hadn't been in the Nam more than a week. We didn't get a chance to talk. They just did a fast patch-up job on me, gave me a knock-out shot and put me on a plane.

It must have been a hell of a shot because I can never remember that plane ride, only going out to the plane. When I came to, they were running me into the operating room at Phu Bai. The doctor was smiling. "I'm gonna give you a little bumble bee bite." Boom. I'm out again.

When I awoke, I found myself in bandages from head to toe. Sully was on one side of me and Skip the gunner was on the other. Skip was short in the Nam, only a month to go when he was badly hit in the stomach. Tubes were running out of his nose and mouth. He kept screaming to the nurses for morphine, for something to kill the pain. Sully wasn't hit as badly. Just a big hole in his ass. He had to lie on his stomach. Whenever Skip would start in, Sully would shout at the medics, "You motherfuckers better give my buddy some shots. That man saved me. You give him a shot, see!"

My pain came every day when they changed the bandages to clean my wounds. The holes were deep and they would dig right down into them. Scraping them out. I nearly cried every time. Once I almost broke a corpsman's hand when I reached for something to grab. If I could have moved, I would have killed that corpsman. There was more pain than when I had been hit.

After two days at Phu Bai, they moved me again. As I was being carried out, we passed my lieutenant doubled up in a wheelchair. No chance to talk. Boom. Another shot and then I was in Danang. That was one hell of a beautiful hospital run by the Air Force. More modern than anything I had ever seen in the States. Sculptures all around the halls and wards. The whole luxurious works. Plus the first round-eyed American woman I had seen in the Nam. Wow. A real woman! But she was butch. Too bad.

At night they moved in a TV for us. All the latest shows and sports from the States. While I was relaxing in front of the tube, I felt for the first time something funny in my feet. I was paralyzed and it scared the shit out of me. I could not move for love or money. Not even wiggle my toes. But there was one cat across the aisle from me who made me realize how lucky I was. He had been hit accidentally with napalm. He was fucked up all over. At least my face was showing. He was nothing but a long tube of bandages and a name.

Then there were the Air Force dudes.

"What are you in for?"

"Diarrhea."

"Bad sinuses."

And we grunts can't even move.

After only two days at Danang, boom, another shot. This time it was a civilian plane down to Cam Ran Bay. It looked like the States. Traffic lights, stop signs, crosswalks, everything. Then a jeep drove by with a mounted M.60 machine gun and I realized that I was still in the Nam. This was only 1967; '68 was the big year for guns in the States.

The hospital at Cam Ran was groovy—American nurses in short white skirts, and lots of sisters. This was my idea of heaven. TV until 1 A.M. It was supposed to go off at 11 P.M., but we would always whisper pleas to the guy on medical watch. He'd leave it on.

It was stateside TV without the commercials. Even saw the Liberty Bowl from Memphis, which made me sick as a dog. The announcer was telling us that we were in beautiful Memphis, Tennessee. The sun is shining and all that good shit. I doubt that they know these games are shown in the Nam. I just lay there and ate my heart out. There was another cat in the ward from Memphis, Hamilton H.S., one of my high school rivals. We beat them in my senior year. I would always ride his ass about that. No Wildcat could ever beat a Lion. Always whipped his ass in checkers too.

There was a movie outside every night. Stretched out on my back, I could never be moved out there. They had to turn me over several times a day. The nurses cleaned my wounds now. One was a real fox. I'd be lying naked in front of her, a little bashful. I could never let myself cry in front of a woman. I'm a Marine! And if I started to scream, she'd remind me that I was a Marine. To which I was always tempted to reply, Fuck off, cunt. But she was also an officer. And there was always that nice soft hand to grab.

She never realized how much it hurt, until I told her. Guess she thought that I was only jiving her for attention. She must have felt sorry for me, because she came around with a shot of morphine every time after that. That was my first and only experience with getting really high. Thirty minutes after that shot, I'm grooving, babe! She'd be cleaning and scraping away, while I grooved.

The Air Force doctors were O.K. They had a lot of sympathy

for grunts. With us they took extra care. After a while they wanted me to walk. But it was impossible. So they'd prop me up in a wheelchair and roll me out into the sun, where I'd fuck around with the Vietnamese peasants. It was a kick to watch these cats the first time they saw a TV. All this music and gunshots coming out of a little box. The little fucker would creep around to the front to see the picture and start babbling away. Then run and bring back about ten of his buddies to see the magic box. The show would last until the corpsman chased them away.

ME AND LYNDON

LBJ, that jolly old turd.

It was December 23, 1967. Almost Christmas in Vietnam. I was in the hospital just about half-dead. Looked like an Egyptian mummy, wrapped neck to toe in white bandages. Combat was a million miles away.

Then all this commotion breaks out. Little people start running all over the ward, pushing beds in and out, scrubbing walls. A real madhouse scene. This has never happened any other morning, so I don't know what the hell is going on.

"What's up, man?"

"The Man is coming today."

"The Man? Who is The Man?"

"The Man. The Big Man."

"You mean LBJ?"

"Yeah, ol' Lyndon's comin' here."

The President is coming to this hospital to see us! This is a big deal. But I'm not going to show it. Me, Whit, I'm cool. Nobody ever gets my ass in this place. The Man. So what. No big thing. If The Man wants to come, let him come. But I was excited, jumping around inside. Like a little kid. Just like every other cat in that ward.

We went back to jiving with our raps until it was about time for The Man to make the scene. Not a hell of a lot to do in a military hospital, even when you're excited. Just lie there and wait.

Boooosh! About a hundred newsmen came bursting through the doors. What's going on, Jack? I'm still in the Nam. I know that much. I thought it was Charlie that done broke loose. Newsmen, TV cameras, lights, everything. Plus, all the dudes who were wounded in action were brought into my ward, so The

Man could pin medals on us. It was a real madhouse. All for LBJ.

The Man comes in. We ain't moving a muscle. He strolls up the aisle. Everybody is wearing shit-eating grins from ear to ear. But me, I'm fighting hard to hold it back. Yeah, I'm still cool. He ain't come to me yet.

Finally The Man gets to my bed. I'm stiff as a board in front of him. He walks up next to me and takes my hand. Just standing there, looking down at me. Looking so sad, as if the whole world were on his shoulders. Right behind him are all these big-ass generals and about a hundred newsmen climbing all over the place. Shining lights and clicking cameras.

Then some dude picks up this sign at the foot of my bed and starts to read it off. "Lance Corporal Terence Marvel Whitmore, Memphis, Tennessee. Wounded December 15, 1967." Blahsie, blahsie, blahsie. LBJ is still holding my hand. I'm trying so hard to stay cool. Ooowhee, the President of the United States is holding my hand. And all I'm doing is yes-sirring him the whole time.

"How do you feel, son?"

"Fine, sir, fine." I'm half-dead. But when The Man asks me how I'm doing, it's just "Fine, sir, fine. Ready to go back to combat. Ready to go back."

"Where you from, son?"

"Tennessee."

"Ya know, I'll bet all those Tennesseans are real proud of you, son. Real proud of you back home."

"Yes sir, thank you, sir. Thank you, sir." Now my voice is really trembling.

It was time to pass out the medals. So The Man went back to get them from this pretty velvet-lined case and walked back to my bed. With every other guy, The Man just pinned them on his pajama top. But he couldn't do the same with me all wrapped up in bandages. There was no pajama top. So he just stood there for a second, smiled a bit.

"Is it all right if I pin your medals on your pillow, son?"

"Oh, yes sir. Yes sir. Anywhere, sir, anywhere."

"I sure hate to see you looking like this, son." Sure he does. Like I know that it's his fault that I'm lying there. But that's not on my mind at this point. Even if it were, I sure as hell was not about to say anything.

The Man pinned the medals on my pillowcase. Shook my hand and all that. Then I glanced over to the other side of my bed and in front of all these tall American newsmen is this little—I didn't know what to call it. About the ugliest little runt I had ever seen. A weasel in shades about five feet five. Pencil mustache. The Man introduces the weasel.

"I'd like you to meet Marshall Ky of the Republic of South Vietnam."

Then Ky started to pump my hand. "Oh, zank you. Zank you very much." The son of a bitch is thanking me because I had my ass shot up just to save his thieving little ass. Now I'm half-dead with a medal on my pillow. Big fucking deal. But I still keep my mouth shut. My President is there. My Commander in Chief.

After The Man moved on to the next bed, the newsmen swooped in on top of me. What's your name? Where you from? What's your daddy's name? What your daddy do? They wanted a whole goddamn autobiography right there on the scene. Before I could answer one question, they were asking another. But it was exciting. I was really grooving on it. Just jumping up and down inside, but never showing it. Me, Whit, and I'm still cool.

"Man, don't be falling all over my bed. I gotta sleep here. Get off my bed, man!"

Westmoreland, the original General Westmoreland, was following behind LBJ. By now he was in front of the dude on my left from the 101st Airborne Division. They were supposed to be hot shit for the Army. So of course the two of us were always jaw-jacking about whose outfit was better. Westmoreland was coming in his pants with this dude from the 101st.

"Son, you just gotta stay out there punchin' and punchin'

and punchin' away. We gonna win this war yet, son." It didn't seem to make any difference to old Westmoreland that this dude's arm was half shot off. He wasn't going to be punching anybody anymore.

At about this time a newsman asked me what unit I'm in. "I'm in One-one." Westmoreland overheard this.

"You in the hundred and first too, soldier?"

"Hundred and first? Man, I'm in One-one. First Marine, First Division. I ain't in no motherfuckin' army! I'm a U. S. Marine!" I was grooving too high to realize who he was. Didn't even notice all the goddamn stars. But he just walked off.

"Man, do you know who that was?" The dude next to me is having a shit fit.

"No. Who?"

"General Westmoreland."

Westmoreland! Goddamn, take me right now, Jack, 'cause I know I'm going to the brig.

GOOD-BYE, NAM!

Christmas came and I was still at Cam Ran Bay. The Red Cross threw one hell of a party for us. One of the doctors, dressed up like Santa Claus, toured the wards on a hospital bed done up like a sleigh. Presents, special food with all the trimmings, the whole Christmas goodies works. After dinner, there were Christmas shows on TV for the rest of the day. But Santa Claus had been the high point of everyone's Vietnam Christmas.

New Year's Eve was another show for the troops. They brought in a group of beautiful Vietnamese girls from Saigon. They gave us special presents made by the Vietnamese for New Year's. This made us feel very good inside even though we weren't at home. It was probably the one and only time we had such good personal contact with Vietnamese people.

That gun team I had helped out at Con Thien was also in the hospital at Cam Ran. We got together that night for a party. The brother whom we had sent out of the hole had been hit in the head with shrapnel from one of the first mortar rounds to be fired at us. He did not want to return to combat when I spoke to him on New Year's Eve. But he expected them to order him back. My heart went out to the guy. But I couldn't help feeling relieved that I was unable to walk back into combat even if they ordered me.

A week after New Year's, they strapped me into a cot and put me in a rack on a huge medical plane. The doc came alongside as they were wheeling me out on the field.

"Look, I got some bad news for you. You know, you got polka-dotted pretty bad. I'm afraid that we have to send you to Japan."

Afraid? The doc had some sense of humor. Bad news, shit! I made him repeat that just to be certain. It was unbelievable. I never thought that I would leave that world of shit. Out of the fucking Nam.

YOKOHAMA, JAPAN

Arriving from Vietnam on a huge Air Force medical troop carrier. I can't see a thing because I'm paralyzed. There are about seventy or eighty other wounded soldiers on the plane.

When we left Nam, it was hot. A blanket was thrown over me and I started to melt. But when we hit Japan and the huge back doors of that plane swung open, the hawk came swooping in. That cold wind cutting like a razor blade.

Next thing I know they're carrying me off the plane. There's some confusion because they haven't made hospital reservations for all the wounded on the plane. The airport is just a reception center with no hospital facilities. Three big Huey choppers are waiting for the most seriously wounded. The first time I had seen a Huey without guns and rockets. No armament anywhere in sight. Now I really felt safe. Back to civilization. Only the cold was getting at me.

The flight to the hospital was a lovely groove. It was early morning in Japan. Barely dawn. And I was struggling to get my first glimpse of Japan. A safe country where no one would be shooting at me. Flashing lights below us. Tokyo. Cars on the highways. Mount Fuji, all orange on the horizon.

And then Kashini Barracks. An Army hospital. Strange place to bring a Marine.

Four wounded guys on the Huey, all getting first-class treatment. Orderlies to pick us up immediately and rush us onto a medical bus where a doctor was waiting to check our conditions and our records. More orderlies with beds waiting for us at the hospital. Stretcher onto the bed and right up to the wards.

"Marine?" Odd looks from the night nurse on duty. "I thought all Marines were tough. What are you doing in a hospital?" They could kid me as much as they liked. I was safe and loving every minute of it. They're only joking. Nobody's shooting at me.

There was a lot of activity when I awoke. All kinds of guys with all kinds of wounds. Questions. Where'd you get it? How'd you get it? Mortar, man. What about you? Paralyzed. Dislocated my spinal cord. How did you do that, man? Playing football.

Playing what? Football. That's the Army for you. Good times in Japan.

The guy on the other side of me still had his helmet with him. His buddies had sent it from the Nam. With a bullet hole in one end, out the other. I had to check that several times. What the hell did his head look like? He caught me staring at him.

"Yeah man, I was lucky."

No shit, you were lucky. He had been caught in an ambush and a ricocheting bullet had passed through his helmet. Not a scratch. He caught his wounds elsewhere.

The doctors came in to beat on me with little hammers and stick me with pins. "Do you feel anything?"

Goddamn I feel something! Must be getting better. It seemed like every doctor in the hospital had to drop by and stick me a few times.

There were all kinds of dudes in the ward. Every day new faces appeared, old ones left. I became especially good raps with a white GI from the 173rd Airborne Division. He caught his at Dakto, the biggest scene in the Nam at that time. A big, bad guy.

"Dakto, man. I got my stuff at Dakto."

He was in charge of me. Showed me the ropes. Helped me eat my meals. Rounded up a wheelchair for me and took me on tours of the hospital and the base. A very good-hearted guy. We hit the base snack bar and movies together. It had been a long time. A long, long time.

A black cat fell in with us and we all became running buddies. They were both badly wounded, but they could walk. They'd push me over to physical therapy and then to the snack bar to catch all the latest sounds. Loved those sounds.

Of course I'd harass them about being Army pussies. They'd call me "jarhead." I'd watch while they tried to shoot a little pool. We were becoming close raps running together like that. Life was a groove.

My doctor didn't come around often after the first day. Got my meals and pain pills. Some physical therapy. Then one day the doctor saw me trying to get up from my wheelchair.

"Keep trying, son. You're not going back to Vietnam. It's all up to you now. How fast you get home depends on you."

That's fine by me, doc. Just what I wanted to hear. Physical therapy would be my ticket home. Soon I was on crutches. Making progress.

My first night on the town! Ooooweee! My white buddy had been getting me up for it. He had been out nearly every night and was supposed to have lined up some broads for us. They were prostitutes but would give free screws for certain guys they liked. Well we didn't groove too much on these hogs. But for a first night out, it wasn't a bad time.

Saturday we hit Yokohama center. Fabulous! Packed with people shopping. No cars. Just lots of lovely people. This is the scene you picture when your friendly local recruiter back on the block gives you the pitch about fun, travel and adventure. But I had to get my ass shot up first to experience it. Yokohama and its happy-go-lucky people. Everybody is shopping and having a ball.

We wanted to spend what little money we had at the Navy PX. Cheapest place in town. Only for Navy and Marine personnel. IDs required to get in. Well, my ID was somewhere back on a battlefield in Vietnam, so the son of a bitch wouldn't let me in. Here I am *on crutches* and this white bastard won't believe that I'm military! The other guys swore to him that I was

a Marine. No go. Bust my balls for these bastards in that stink-
ing war and then they won't even let me in their PX! My only
thought was that at that very moment my buddies were getting
shot up in the Nam while these dudes are living off the tit in
Japan. Fuck 'em, I'll give my business to the Japanese.

We hopped a cable car to Chinatown. The car was packed
with Japanese. Lovely people. Lovely? There she was. The first
time I laid eyes on her. Taki with her books sitting in a corner.
Couldn't take my eyes off her. She got off after a few stops. I'm
right behind her.

"Where you goin', Whit? This ain't our stop."

I could care less. Right on her tail. Right back to the shopping center. She disappeared into a little place called "Peanuts."
Sat down at her table.

"You speak English?"

Not a word from her. Just all smiles. "Soul Man" by Wilson
Pickett was on the box.

"Young lady, can you dance?"

She was too shy. Well, I'm a go-getter for dancing. Cut in on
two girls dancing together. This one could speak a little English
with a hell of an effort. But it was enough of an effort to arouse
Taki's interest.

"You dance very well."

"You speak English? Why didn't you tell me. C'mon, baby,
I'm gonna show you how to dance too."

Well, that started it. No stopping us now. We made plans to
meet next weekend, my only time off for liberty.

We were flying high that night on our way back to the ward.
Feeling no pain. Except for the ward nurse.

"Keep your voices down."

"Aw, let us be, will ya?"

"You're forgetting my rank, soldier. Get in your racks."

Dumb cunt. She squealed on us. I had to appear before a
Marine liaison officer the next morning. It all came back. The
dirty, nasty Marine Corps. I was leading a groovy Army life.

No DIs breathing down my back twenty-four hours a day. Now there it was again, staring me right in the face. He jumped in my shit but good. I wasn't prepared for any boot lieutenant ordering me to get a haircut and shave my mustache.

As the female barber was doing a proper military job on my head, I spotted a familiar face in the mirror. My lieutenant from Con Thien. Walking! He recognized me immediately. Grabbed me around the shoulders. He must have forgotten all his Marine Corps training. He didn't even call me "trooper."

"Son, I'll never forget your face. How are you, son? What the hell is your name? I can't forget that face, but your name slips me."

"Whit, sir."

He was in his greens. On his way home. Stateside. But he expected to return to the Nam again for a full thirteen months' tour. I had a lot more time than he had in the military and Nam, so this made me even more confident that I'd be going home soon and getting a medical discharge.

The liaison officer had me switched to a ward where the guys were in better shape. Roll call every morning. Occasionally pull a detail. But it was still the Army. Lots of free time. Shoot pool. Listen to soul at the snack bar.

My pay records from Nam caught up with me at this point. All that back pay which I had never spent. Right in my pocket. Ooooweee! Party time. Downtown to have me a ball. Found me three of the best-looking hookers and had a time. Got it all out of my system. Crutches, limp and all, there was no stopping me.

After I had my fill of them, I split for a late-night stroll around town. A cab pulled up alongside.

"What you want, GI? Smokes. Girls. What you want?"

Well, I certainly didn't want a cab, but now that I'd caught my breath I thought I'd try on some new broads for size. He takes me to some back alley and in steps this lady. A woman, not a girl. She ain't exactly a beauty contest winner. This is the first time I'm shelling out dough for an older woman.

"She O.K.?"

"Yeah, I guess so."

Giving her the hairy eyeball up and down. She better know some good tricks. Like twenty dollars' worth of good tricks.

Up to her apartment. Weird? I mean it is weird. She's a Buddhist and she had these goddamn statues all over the place. One of them with smoke coming out of his balls.

She saw me staring and started to tell me about Buddha. It was hypnotic. That broad could really rap. I wasn't even thinking about sex tricks anymore. Just staring right into her eyes and grooving on Buddha. She knew her shit. About Christ, about the Bible. I just sat there with my jaws hanging for about two hours. Then she fell into her thing.

Weeeaaaw—what an act! Easily worth twenty dollars. She laid me down. On my back. One piece of clothing off at a time. My clothing. She's already down to these teeny weeny bra and panties.

One piece at a time as she stands over me. But no touchee. Only lookee. Then she starts rubbing me. She rubs every goddamn muscle in my body. I mean *every* muscle. Most of them just go right to sleep. Then she walks up and down right on top of me. Digging her toes into me. Aaaarrrgh!! She's got nothing on now. . . . And I'm staring up at it. . . . There it is! Right over me. . . . Right up there. . . . And I can only stare at it. I'm so relaxed, I can't even move. . . . Can't even touch it. Whew!

Then she sits on me. Yaaaagh!!!

Relief. A lot more than twenty dollars' worth. These Japanese women sure know how to treat a man.

Made it back to the base just in time to fall in for 7 A.M. roll call. Then back to town in the afternoon. Party. Same scene, every day, every night. Until Saturday. Time to meet Taki at "Peanuts."

"Don't be shy. Let's dance."

She grabbed my hand and headed for the door. Where we goin'? Everywhere. We walked all over town. To some of the most beautiful parks I'd ever seen. Up to the top of a grassy hill overlooking the docks of Yokohama. Just watching the ships until nightfall. And that first kiss. Let's had it up, baby! Back to her pad for the night.

What a pad! Western style in a mixed Japanese, European and American neighborhood. She was a university student and part-time clothes model. So she had some bread.

The walls were covered with sculptures and paintings. And this wild poster of a black man and a white man. One is right side up. The other is upside down. And they're biting each other's feet. What the hell? People know about our problems even outside the States. That was the first time I realized it. And then there was a photo of Martin Luther King. A cartoon of the President: "Hey, hey, LBJ, how many kids did you kill today?" "Make love, not war." The whole scene. My first contact up close with anything anti-American. I didn't know how to react.

She fixed some tea for us. And we started to rap about black people in America, my home, my family. And Vietnam. About the war.

"Did you actually kill people in Vietnam?"

"Yeah, a few." I didn't want to talk about it. "The American-Japanese war is over. Americans are fighting in Nam now. Your people have nothing to do with it." I didn't want to talk anymore.

Time for our love scene. The bathtub. Japanese bathtubs are fantastic! They're not long, but deep. Deep enough to stand up in. Groovy. She was washing me. I washed her. Then into the sack. I ain't telling no more about that.

Split in a hurry early that morning. Had to find a cab to get back to the base by 7 A.M. Fat chance. A big American Pontiac came cruising down the street with a Spec. 5 Army medic from my ward behind the wheel. Naturally he takes his time driving across Yokohama. So I'm half an hour late. My ass chewed out again.

Back to the old weekday routine. Roll call. Pulling details. Shoot pool. Wait for the weekend. Then at one morning's roll call.

"Corporal Terry Whitmore, orders."

I almost fell through the floor. Five stories down to the bottom. He gave me orders home to Bethesda Naval Hospital! I moved as fast as I could to the office where guys were cleared for leaving the base. Orders right in my hand. All I could think about was going home to Memphis!

The office was packed with guys waiting to go home. So I started to decipher my orders. U. S. Navy? What the hell is that doing in my orders? I'm in the USMC. What is this shit, man?

I'm chewing on my heart by this time. Don't even want to look at the name. Jerry Whitemore. Corpsman. I ain't no goddamn corpsman! These dumb bastards. They're fucking with me again. Why me? I'm about ready to cry.

Back to the sergeant on my ward.

"Sergeant, you called me out this morning. Are these my orders?"

"Whitemore. Jerry Whitemore. Is that you?"

"Hell no, it ain't me."

"No big thing. Guess I made a mistake."

Made a mistake? You dumb motherfucker! There's no description of what I wanted to do to him. That fucked me up for the rest of the day.

Taki and I were supposed to meet again that night. She had never been to Chinatown. The Japanese lived all around it but never went there. It was full of GIs, merchant seamen and foreigners.

We rode down in the cable car from her apartment. Off to find a new place. The Club 45. This was where it was at!

Where It's At, Baby! *Stone soul.* Funky music. Smoky. And smelling of chitlins. Chitlins! In Japan.

Slapping hands with all my brothers. Heaven. Two huge plates full of chitlins for me and Taki. Just one of those mellow nights when everything goes right.

It was all new for Taki. Black slang and GI English. Soul food and funky music. She's grooving on it. And starting to dig me. Of course I'm loving every minute of it. After that we saw each other almost every night.

But soul dancing was something she couldn't handle. Too shy for all that body action. I had to teach her from scratch. At night in private. She had a small record player. Layed a little soul on it.

"Ya gotta move everything, baby."

"I'm moving . . . I'm moving."

Like a sack of flour. Nothing is happening. Try a new angle.

"When we make love, how do you move?"

"Oh, like this, of course."

"Now just put a little more into it. Get more parts moving."

"Yes, like make love. Just like make love?"

Fell right into it, babe. No stopping us now. A few more nights of "make love" like this and she was hot to trot. Wanted to get out and show everybody just what she was into. She took me to downtown Yokohama to one of her old student hangouts. No GIs or brothers there. Just young Japanese. This was meant to be a real premiere.

The joint had a jukebox and a postage-stamp-size dance floor. But there wasn't much going down on that floor. Taki was impatient so she dropped some yen in the jukebox for a little soul time. Back off, baby, 'cause we're going to it!

The floor was all ours. Everybody, but everybody, got off that floor to watch us. That bartender was giving us free drinks just to keep the show going. She was that fucking good. Knocked her old buddies for a loop.

"We make love. We make love."

She's whispering this to me all the time we're dancing. Gettin'

in that groove. Goddamn, just wait 'til the brothers check out
my new soul sister!

"Git it. baby. . . . Git it, brother. . . . Do your thing, babe,
do your thing."

The Club 45 was going out of its suck. We were doing our
thing together and every one was lapping it up.

Dancing wasn't my only freak scene. *Movies.* I hadn't seen
any in the Nam except for an occasional Western or a John
Wayne flick. Taki was also a film nut, so we hit every new
flick in town. In English, of course. One flick we caught was
The Fox, a movie about some lesbian broads. Taki was flipping
out watching some guy take one of these women into a barn
and all kinds of love noises are coming at us, even though the
lovers really can't be seen. Those noises got our imaginations
going. He was really socking it to that lessie.

"Let's go home."

She's grabbing my hand. Taki can't wait to get at it.

"Goddamn, keep your voice down, babe. We gonna get home
soon."

Loved that chick. She was always so honest. I called her
dumb. But it was just honesty.

Then she brought me into her thing. Nature. She was a great
outdoors freak. Turning me on to every hill and park around
Yokohama. And they had some lovely, lovely spots. Every
Saturday and Sunday afternoon Taki packed a picnic and we'd
head for the hills. Our favorite was packed with little kids.
Just kids running all over the place. This was their territory
and we were guests. A big black man playing for hours with
all these tiny Japanese kids. Going out of my nut on swings,
slides, monkey bars. What a scene! I hadn't felt so completely
relaxed or enjoyed myself so much in years. Just a few more
weeks and I'd be bouncing around with my little brothers and
sisters in the same way. And my new daughter. The real world
was getting more real all the time.

And my legs and arm were regaining their strength. Dancing. Hikes in those hills. Even making love. All of it was getting me back in shape. And of course physical therapy every weekday.

There was a wonderful woman therapist. A Navy lieutenant and German immigrant. Red hair and a fantastic build like all these Nordic broads. She smiled and coaxed me through those exercises. That tender smile and her touch had been my first real feminine contact after the Nam. I had started therapy before I met Taki. First this lieutenant was picking me up from my wheelchair. Soon we were working out on the exercise bars. Then my crutches. Of course I was nuts about this chick. So were at least fifty other guys she had helped to walk again. Getting them back home faster.

The stronger my legs became, the more I got around. And the more I got around, the closer I got to home. Or more exactly, to the States. That good ol' American way of life was sneaking back up on me. Taki never said a word to me about it. She kept her mouth shut when hillbilly lifers would make cracks about us. A mixed couple. It really gave them the ass. Her eyes were almost round and she had fair skin. Even at a close distance, she could pass for white.

During one evening of touring the base snack bars and bowling alleys, we caught enough wisecracks and bad eyes from white dudes to keep us as far away from the military as much as possible. Taki was afraid of soldiers anyway. She'd always cuddle up close to me whenever GIs were around. But the inside of a military base was something she had never seen. She forced me to take her there to satisfy her curiosity. One night was enough satisfaction, enough of a lesson in the American way of life. After that night, we tried to keep to ourselves in Yokohama. Rarely hitting the off-base GI bars, even the Club 45.

We thought we had found one place away from the usual GI scene. Taki and I were sitting quietly in this gin mill. My black buddy was bullshitting with the bartender who was buying him drinks to keep his company. Three white drunks came busting in. On R and R from the Nam.

"Hey, Jap, you give me a cold beer, ya hear, boy!"

The bartender didn't give him any back talk. Just gave him his beer. That didn't satisfy these white dudes.

"Boy, you look just like those gooks I been fighting back in Nam. And you know what, boy? I'm going back to kill me some more gooks like you."

"Hey man, the bartender ain't messing with you. Why don't you leave him alone?"

The brother was being very polite about it. But these dudes kept on fucking with the bartender. Taki was learning again. With that school look on her face. Not saying a word, just soaking it all in.

"Now you leave him alone. You asked for a drink and he gave you one. What more do you want?"

"Ain't nobody talkin' to you. We're just having fun with this gook. All these motherfuckers are the same. Just fuckin' gooks. Japanese. Chinese. Vietnamese. They're all slanty-eyed li'l bastards."

The brother was paralyzed in his right arm, but he wasn't about to take any more from these dudes.

"That's enough shit. Now just get the fuck out."

Who is this nigger? It was all over their faces. They turned and moved to the door. But they mumbled loud enough for us to hear them.

"Things sure are getting fuckin' bad anytime a nigger sticks up for a Jap!"

Kabaaaw! That dude was flying out the door and sliding on his ass across the snow. The brother had let him have it with his good arm. He was a hard ass, hard-core block black from Philadelphia.

"Wait, wait man. Why the hell are we fightin' each other? We're all Americans, right? If we're supposed to be fightin' anybody, we should be kicking these Jap gooks in the ass!"

Taki was standing right up next to me. This must have really hurt her. Now it's my fight too. I jumped off the bar stool with my foot right up the dude's ass.

"You haul your fuckin' asses outta here and don't let me see your ugly motherfuckin' faces around here no more!"

We were two very angry brothers.

"Look at this shit we have to go through! We catch it at home and we have to catch it over here too. Look at me! My goddamn arm is no good no more and you're walkin' around on crutches. We must be motherfuckin' crazy! I ain't takin' no more shit from these white motherfuckers. Next time I'm gonna kill me one!!"

Taki was all eyes and shaking like a leaf. She had had another lesson. But it wasn't going to be the last. It had been no small shock for me either. Americans versus Americans. Goddamn, I *must* be getting close to home!

Too close. It was only a few days later that Yokohama was invaded by the U. S. Navy. An aircraft carrier was in port and five thousand squids were on liberty. All over the town, nothing but these goddamn marshmallow hats with drunks underneath them. The carrier had been off Nam for a few months, so they were all war heroes. Wasn't a goddamn one of them who had seen a day of combat. Except maybe their pilots. And all they do is ride high and push buttons.

Taki and I were with my white buddy this time. She was sitting on my stool between my legs. The only girl in the place. It was just a quiet after-hours bar. No hustlers.

"Hey, bartender, where's all yo' gals at?"

A cracker. A goddamn loud-mouth cracker. Just what we need to ruin a good evening.

"We all just come in from the coast of Vietnam. Five months in that shit. Y'all sure got it nice 'n' lucky over here in Japan. It's damn hot in Nam."

Ain't nobody saying nothing. Every cat in the place is a wounded combat vet. Just sitting there, listening to this squid's bullshit about Nam . . . and girls.

"Aw c'mon, bartender, where you hidin' all them pretty things?"

"We have no girls. No girls work in this bar."

"Hey, what you talkin' 'bout? That's a girl. Right over there."

He's pointing at Taki. Then he notices me.

"Goddamn, will ya'll look at that Jap. What she done got herself?"

"Jarhead, that sounds like Injun talk to me."

A real motherfucking instigator. My white buddy is just itching to have a brawl with these four squids. Nobody liked the Navy.

"Hey, squid, don't you know that everyone in here is a wounded vet from Nam?"

"Y'all been to Nam?"

Now they were a little scared. They knew that they were aggravating a bar full of combat vets.

"Why hell, we all been to Vietnam too. We all vets in here, right?"

Somebody put some sounds on the jukebox to break the tension.

It didn't help. I don't know who started the fight, but it started. Pile on in. Tables turning. Chairs flying. Those goddamn squids were all in uniform, so there was no trouble telling the teams apart.

Headed right for that cracker and sent him crashing into the jukebox. I was hookin' but good. We had those Navy boys wrapped up.

"SP comin'!"

Shore Patrol. The bartender didn't waste any time in calling them. Dudes were flying out every door and window in the place. Shit was erupting!

Taki dragged me to the back of the bar. This is my girl. We're drinking. Minding our own business. We don't know anything.

The man broke in and turned on all the lights. Billy clubs and .45s. Big, mean boys.

They were picking up the squids, while we had it out the door and split in a cab.

"Terry, why are you Americans so crazy? Why do you always fight?"

I'd be goddamned if I could answer her.

Even my two buddies began to throw sparks at each other— racist sparks. They never came to blows, because I'd always come between them and try to humor them out of a fight. I couldn't see any good reason why the three of us, all running buddies, all wounded in Nam, should have to slug it out. But these two were getting closer to it every day. They had to be split.

Taki and I took the white dude out with us. Get him away from the bar-girl scene and fix him up with one of Taki's student friends. She was a cute chick. Short and plump but a great sense of humor. And she kept this white dude in his place. Wouldn't let him touch her. Now it was my turn to laugh at these Army lovers.

We took them home to Taki's pad for a traditional Japanese dinner.

"Can we give you girls some help?"

"No, no. No help. You must leave kitchen."

Just what I was waiting to hear. She didn't have to say it twice. Like I said, I really grooved on those Japanese traditions. Very civilized!

After dinner and tea, we all sacked out for the night. It was one long battle between the two of them.

"No. We must know each other better."

"Goddamn, we been together all day!"

Taki and I were cracking up. He crept over to me in the middle of the night.

"I'm so fucking horny, man. What the hell did you fix me up with? She just don't give!"

Poor bastard. That's your problem. I could tell this was coming and it tickled the hell out of me. Earlier that evening, she had been staring every which way at that poster of the black man and white man munching on each other's feet.

"Taki, bbblllbbblll?"

In Japanese. Taki giggled and shook her head "no."

"What's she saying? What's so funny about that poster?"

"She thinks they're doing sixty-nine."

So I just knew my white buddy was going to have a rough time with that chick.

That next morning, the four of us went out to the park. It was a quiet, cold day. It was the first time I was really twisted inside about the war and I was scared. The three of us often jived each other about never going back to the Nam.

"No man, I ain't that crazy. There's no reason in the world for going back into that shit."

But if the orders had come, we'd go. Of course we'd never admit that to each other.

We climbed a steep hill overlooking the entire port of Yokohama. It was cold, so Taki had brought along a thermos of coffee and a blanket. The four of us were cuddled under the blanket, cozy and warm, sipping our coffee in this Japanese lovers' park. Nobody was saying a word. But we were close. All thinking the same things. All hugged up under each other. Not in Nam, not in the States had we ever been together with people of different colors like this. And the chances of it happening again were pretty slim. It sure as hell wasn't going to be like this when we got home. These were my thoughts and I know that the other three were thinking along the same lines.

"Hey, look at that liner down there. Must be taking all those tourists home."

Home. The atmosphere was getting to my white buddy.

"Jarhead, we ain't gonna be doin' much of this together when we get back home. Just think, man, we were killing all these people here just twenty-five years ago. Bombing the hell out of them. Now we ain't never had it so good. I bet you we be doin' the same things in Hanoi in ten years. Partying with all them Vietnamese."

"No man, there ain't gonna be nuthin' left in Hanoi, the way we goin' at them now."

The girls hadn't said a word, but this let them loose on us.

"Why can't you be like this in America? Why must you kill each other in America and in Vietnam? You never tell us why."

"Do you really kill people?"

Now it was getting out of hand. We had to change the subject. Sure I was thinking about these things. We're killing in Nam. We're killing in the States. But if I start to think about *why*, I'm going to turn. I'm military, I can't afford to do that. If I start thinking about why, I know I'm in trouble.

"Let's go party in Chinatown."

Why? Goddamnit, don't ask me why. I don't know.

HAPPY BIRTHDAY, GRUNT

March 6, 1968.

My birthday. To be exact, my twenty-first. Now you're a man, son. Old enough to drink beer back in the States.

Taki knew about it and was preparing a surprise birthday party for me. Baked a cake. Presents. It was supposed to have been a double celebration. Not only was I going to be twenty-one, but I had been off crutches for a while by this time. We both knew that I'd soon be getting my orders to return home.

The night before, I had decided to stay in bed, just get some rest before all that partying. At ten o'clock my doctor came strolling in. This was a strange hour for him to be visiting a patient. Even stranger was that he hadn't said a word to me since January. Not since he had encouraged me to start walking again. So I knew something big had to be up.

Every day some dude on the ward would be going home.

"Take it easy, Whit. Be seein' ya!"

"Soon, babe, soon. I'm comin' right behind you."

Now it had to be my turn. This is for real. I'm gonna be hadding it up! Goin' home, babe, I just know it.

"Whitmore, how are you doing?"

"I'm getting along fine, sir. Real fine."

"Yes, we've noticed that. Your records have been checked over and you appear to be in tip-top condition. So I think we'll be sending you back to Vietnam."

Just like that. Back to Vietnam.

I lay back on my bed. No reaction from me. He had knocked me cold without laying a hand on me.

"You'll be getting your orders in the morning. You're in A-1 condition, Whitmore."

And he walked out.

Combat. All I could see was swamps . . . humping up and down those hills . . . my buddies getting shot up . . . those poor kids crying their eyes out . . . I'm ducking bullets.

No, doc, you don't mean me. Not me. No more of that shit for me. What the hell kind of fucking birthday present is this? No, goddamnit, I didn't like it one bit, I didn't want it, but I knew that I'd do it. I'd go back to Vietnam. Getting my orders in the morning. Wasn't a fucking thing I had to say or do about it.

Fuck it. I jumped out of my rack, into my clothes and split for a cab. Off to Taki's pad. With only a few hours left, we had better start partying now.

"What are you doing here? I thought you were staying in tonight."

"I, unh, got some news tonight."

She knew, but she didn't know exactly when. I was none too happy, so she suspected the worst.

"I gotta go back."

Not a word from her. Tears in her eyes but not a word. She made some of the usual Japanese green tea. We ate my birthday cake. In silence.

"Terry, let's go out. Let's go where there are many people."

Hopped on a cable car downtown, where we ran into some of her friends. She told them the news.

"No, no. You can't go back! You shot, you can't fight."

They weren't bullshitting, or just trying to be nice. They were really sincere about wanting to keep me there, keep me alive. One girl, a mixed breed, grabbed me and put her hands on my head.

"You keep head down. You no die, O.K.?"

"Hell, I got an R and R coming up soon. I'll be back to Japan. We'll party again."

"O.K., but you no die."

"Naw, I'm superman. I can't die."

This was getting to be too much for me. If I stayed around

any longer, I'd be crying my eyes out. These poeple were too good to me.

"Taki, I want to be alone with you. Let's go back home."

We made love very slowly. It was so quiet. And sad. I knew it was the last time. And I was dumb enough to let her know.

"Taki, you have to wake me early in the morning so I can catch the bus."

"What bus? Where you going tomorrow? You go to Vietnam tomorrow?"

Then the shit hit the fucking fan.

Sooner or later it had to be told. But I had planned to work up to it. Prepare her, and myself, for the shock.

"Yeah, Taki, I got to go back tomorrow. Have to catch the plane for Nam."

She went right to it. For the first time she really laid it on.

"Why you black people fight? You don't fight for yourselves. What does America do for you?"

For me? I don't know. *To* me—now that's a different story. She had me. There wasn't any defense for me to give, because she was right on every count. She went on for about a half-hour nonstop, without a word from me. There was nothing for me to say.

"Goddamnit, Taki, I'm military. They gave me my orders, now I have to go back."

"You military? You crazy."

O.K., so I'm just a crazy, dumb nigger, but what the hell else am I going to do?

"Your American way of life is so good? Why you have to kill people to take it? If it so good, you don't have to shoot people to make them take it."

Common sense. I know it. Taki started to cry.

"You die. You never come back to Taki. Never come back to Japan."

"Don't talk like that, Taki. Please don't. I have to think about coming back, else I ain't never gonna make it."

She cried herself to sleep.

In the morning, we caught a cab to Yokohama center. She wasn't saying a word all the way. Just holding me tight as she stared out the window.

"You wait here while I check when the bus leaves."

Taki grabbed me, kissed me and hopped out of the cab. She didn't even look back. Just kept on walking into Yokohama center. Into the morning shopping crowd.

O.K., man, let's go. I'm back in the saddle again. No time for crying. I'm on my way. Had to put her out of my mind or I'd go crazy. Just another groovy war story to tell the brothers back on the block. When I was a kid I used to listen to the older guys, the old vets, in the barber shop tell stories about Korea and the second world war. About all the foreign broads they had in every country. An old vet's story. I'd just have to turn it into one of those and forget the rest.

At the hospital, I put on my fatigues for the first time in months. It was a lousy feeling getting into the green shit again.

Big, bad Marine going back to war. First stop was the base snack bar to meet some other grunts and get back in the mood. Then pick up several copies of my orders. With all my usual bullshitting around, I managed to miss the bus to the airport. Back to the snack bar to kill time until the next one. There I met my first Black Muslim.

"Hey, brother, what's happening?"

I was the only black in the snack bar, so of course he sat down to shoot the shit with me. He was a squid in civvies—with an earring in his ear. So I knew he had to be one of those wild cats I'd heard so much about.

"Where you headin', brother?"

"On my way back to Nam."

"Yeah? That ain't your place, brother."

"What do you mean it ain't my place?"

"Just that. It ain't our place."

"You in the military?"

"Yeah, the Navy."

He was military all right, but he had never been anywhere but Japan. Not Nam, not Okinawa, nowhere but Japan.

"I'm exempted from all that combat shit. I'm a Black Muslim."

Exempted? What the hell is this cat bullshitting about? I ain't ever heard of Black Muslims being exempt from combat. Goddamn, you got any applications for me to sign? This sounds like a good club to join.

But he didn't psych me out. I was still gung-ho American and Marine. He may have been exempt, but it wasn't just because he was a Black Muslim. Mohammed Ali is a Black Muslim and he's still fighting to stay out of the military for religious reasons. No, this cat was just a hot motherfucker whom the Navy wanted out of the way and out of trouble, so they just let him sit in Japan with that earring in his ear.

"Hey, don't you hang out at the Forty-five with a good looking Japanese girl?"

"Yep, that's me."

"You goin' away and leavin' all that?"

"Yep. Got to."

"You're crazy."

He had his wife with him in Japan. They planned on staying there forever and becoming Japanese citizens.

"You know my girl Taki? Well, you just keep an eye on her. Tell her I'm O.K. and I'll be coming back soon."

"Sure thing, brother."

The next bus was in. Threw all my shit in it and climbed aboard. Inside, there was one black cat with his finger wrapped in a cast. We sat together.

"Blood, sweat and tears again, baby. Motherfuckin' mosquitoes . . ."

I was thinking out loud about Nam. He looked at me like I was some kind of nut.

"What you talkin' about, brother?"

"Nam, baby, Nam."

Shook his head.

"Not for me. I'm goin' home. First to Okinawa and then straight home. No more of that jungle shit for me, babe."

Now all this is beginning to piss me off. Isn't anybody going back to the Nam but me? That Spec. 5 sure as hell isn't. The same son of a bitch corpsman from my ward was on the bus with his Japanese wife. He hated my ass because I stayed away from the ward to run around with Taki. I'm certain that it was the Marine liaison officer and this Spec. 5 Army corpsman who fixed it for me to return to the Nam. No, I was none too happy on that bus ride.

The airport was enormous. A good half-hour's bus ride from the base entrance to the terminal. If all the U.S. bases in Japan are that size, Sam must own half the country.

Chaos in the terminal. Thousands of cats in uniform crawling all over the place. Where do we check in? What line should I get on? When does the plane leave? Where can I take a leak?

One of the brothers from the Club 45 had caught the first bus that morning and was already on line.

"Hey man, what's happening?"

"You just get on that line over there and show them your orders."

I stood on the end of a long line. The white dude in front of me was jawjacking with the guy in back of me.

"You mind if I go ahead of you so's I can sit side by side with my buddy?"

"Go ahead. Don't make no difference to me."

By the time I reached the desk, a hell of a lot of guys had checked in to fly back to the Nam. The squid at the desk read my orders and started to run his finger up and down all kinds of lists.

"That's it. Ain't no more seats."

"What you talking about, no more seats?"

"Just what I said. There ain't no more seats on any of the planes today. You have to wait until tomorrow."

I still didn't understand him. What the hell am I going to do now? I got orders to Nam. I have to go there now. Can't be hanging around Japan. The last plane was boarding, so there wasn't much I could do but follow the man's advice and head for the overnight barracks.

My buddy from the Club 45 had to catch the last plane.

"When you get to Okinawa tomorrow, you bug on down to the Four Corners and we catch you there. Take care, brother."

"If they don't send me direct to the crotch, I'll see you on Oki tomorrow."

The Four Corners was *the* soul bar on Okinawa. Nothing but blacks. We would party there for those last few nights before catching a plane to Nam. Had to wait around Oki at least two days.

"Bus for the barracks leaving now."

Had it up, babe. I ain't sleeping in the terminal. Another half-hour ride to the overnight barracks. The squids passed out blankets and sheets. I went to making my bed. When all my shit was straight, it was only six o'clock. What the hell was I going to do for the rest of the night?

"What's happening on this base, man?"

"Just some jive-time club. Not a goddamn thing in the town either."

So I started bullshitting with the squid on the door.

"Hey man, can we leave this barracks? Can we leave the base?"

"If you're on orders, you can go wherever the hell you want as long as you get to where you're supposed to be going on time. You can leave."

Groovy.

"Say, unh, can you spot me a few bucks, 'cause I ain't got no money and I'm supposed to be going back to the Nam tomorrow."

"Here, take five. You've been shot up there once, ain't you?"

He had seen the photo of me and LBJ when I unpacked some of my gear.

"Yeah, I was wounded in combat."

Big, tough guy. But the hustle got me some money for that one last chance—I could see Taki again! I didn't know how the hell I was going back to Yokohama, but goddamn, I had a whole night and morning to be with her and I wasn't pissing it away in Sam's barracks.

"Hey, Navy, how do I get to Yokohama?"

"It's a long ride on the train. You catch it in town."

I'm gone. It might have been a big base, but I was at that front gate in no time. Cocky-ass Marine private on guard duty.

"Where do you think you're going?"

"Out man. I'm on orders, so I'll be back tomorrow morning."

"Let's see your pass."

"Goddamn, I don't need no pass. I told you I'm on orders. I ain't stationed at this base, so I don't need no motherfucking pass."

Showed this hillbilly clown my orders. Six or seven pages of it and he starts to read it line for fucking line. I'm about to rap him in the mouth and take off.

"Yeah, I guess you can go."

Goddamn right I could. And I did, fast as I could to the train station, where all the signs were in Japanese. There were about three platforms, six trains—which one went to Yokohama?

"Yokohama? Which way to Yokohama?"

Everybody was Japanese. Nobody spoke English and they were all staring at me like I was crazy. A train pulled in.

"Yokohama? Yokohama?"

"Yokohama. Yokohama."

Central Station, Yokohama. Lovely. Dashed out into the traffic and grabbed a cab.

"Club 45."

If I had been thinking, I'd have gone to Taki's house, but my mind was running every which way. "Club 45" was just a reflex action. A very lucky one. It was like a corny old flick on the Late Show, because there she was sitting in our old back-of-the-bar seat at the 45. All alone.

Bust in the door and eyeball the place.

"Whit, what the hell you doin' here?"

Taki looked up when she heard the brothers at the bar rapping with me. Like a kangaroo. Out from behind the table. Up into my arms. Ooooweee—it's heaven, baby!

We split for the Piano Bar, a tiny joint without all the noise. An old friend of Taki's was there. Paul. A Japanese cat. He took us out to a few places and back to Taki's pad. He didn't say much after he heard that I was going back to Nam. But at the end of the night, he took off his long, old-fashioned watch chain and broke it into three pieces. One piece he put around my neck, another around my wrist. The third piece went around his neck.

"Brother. We brothers. Be good to yourself. Come back to us."

He had his arms around me. I was about to break out crying when he split.

Taki and I sacked out. I'm trying not to think about it as a lucky last night but just any ordinary night with Taki. She didn't say much to me. The fact that I would return to Nam seemed inevitable to her by now.

But not to me. Doubt had, of course, been building up in my mind for a long time. But now it was stronger than ever. I tried to think of a good reason to return to all that killing in the Nam. Other than the fact that I was a Marine, I couldn't come up with one.

Paul came by early in the morning and the three of us climbed in a cab headed for the airport. It was a long ride, but Taki insisted on taking a cab and paying the bill. She slept on my shoulder almost all the way to the gate.

"Look man, I'm going back to the Nam today and these two very good friends of mine would like to come on base with me. Is it all right?"

"I guess it's O.K."

We drove to the terminal, where I checked in.

"When does the plane leave?"

"It leaves when it gets here and it ain't here yet. You got about a two-hour wait."

Taki, Paul and I chowed down in the snack bar. They were grooving on the sights around a military base. I guess it was a strange place to anyone used to the outside world, although nothing is strange once a person is in the military. They were barraging me with questions. Everything was either unbelievable or laughable or both.

Then the announcement came over the p.a. system and it was only unbelievable.

"Now hear this. Now hear this. All flights for Okinawa have been canceled for today. Repeat."

You didn't have to repeat a goddamned thing. It had already hit me like a ton of bricks. I had to get out of Japan! Get on a plane fast . . . get away from Taki . . . away from Paul, every-body . . . get away from asking myself questions I can't answer . . . just get the fuck back to being a Marine, being in the crotch, doing what I'm told to do and not thinking a goddamned thing about it. Now what the hell am I going to do? There ain't no way out of here today. I guess that was the beginning of the end.

"You stay? You stay?"

"Be quiet. I have to think about what I'm gonna do. C'mon, I'll take you on a tour."

Had to do something to keep them busy. To keep them—and me—from asking questions. Bowling alleys, movies, snack bars, recreation centers. And everywhere we went, it was the same old shit about "Goddamn Japs using our pool tables" or "Can't that Jap stop making so much noise on our piano?" Fuck it. We'd just walk around outside.

Right in front of two squids waiting for a bus, Taki wrote in the gravel road: "Hey, hey, LBJ, how many kids did you kill today?" But when they saw what she wrote, they only smiled. I expected them to at least call for the MPs.

"I better keep you two walking so you stay out of trouble."

As we walked, we came closer and closer to the front gate.

"Where's your pass?"

That same ball-breaking hillbilly private from the night before.

"I told you last night, man, I'm on orders so I don't need no pass."

"But I have to see . . ."

You have to see shit. We're leaving. Dumb, thickheaded hillbilly.

We walked about twenty yards past the gate and I turned around for a last look. Nothing was said. Not even to myself would I admit it. But I felt it deep down inside that I'd never be seeing this place again. Sayonara. It was all out in front of me now. The whole world was waiting for me out there in the night.

START RUNNING

"Goddamn, you back again? You're supposed to be gone, man."

"Whit's too slick. They ain't fast enough to hang on to me."

The brothers at the 45 couldn't believe their eyes. An extra night away from the Nam was lucky enough. But coming back again . . . who is this masked man? They knew something was up, but I was in no mood to start rapping about it.

All this shit is heavy on my mind now. I'm very uptight. Scared. Don't even want to talk to Taki, much less to the brothers. We left the 45 for home and bed. It had been a long day for Taki. She was sound asleep in no time. But me—what the hell am I going to do? At ten o'clock in the morning, I have to be at Sam's terminal to get on one of his planes back to the Nam. Sweet dreams.

Sam has put me through a lot of shit—and I can't even say why. Not only can't I come up with some good excuses for Sam to be wiping out the Vietnamese people, but I can't even think of one good reason for me to help Sam in his dirty work. Yeah, I'm an American and a Marine and a black man, so when the man says go, I go. I've always gone, no questions asked. But this time there are questions: Why did that happen with Bravo Company and everybody treating it like a big joke? Why are a couple of million Americans flying back and forth to Nam year after year with all their huge planes, ships, tanks, bombs, computers, whore houses—just to kick every yellow ass in the Nam? To help the Vietnamese people? Hell, I just helped them to commit suicide, that's all. But no, Sam wasn't going to send me back in after I caught that mortar round for him. No sir, I was a war hero! LBJ himself gave me some nice shiny medals for my good work and with those medals and a quarter I could get a beer at the PX snack bar. Big fucking deal! Did the man keep his word? *No*—you're in A-1 condition, Whitmore, so we're sending you back to Vietnam! *Why* are you sending me back? Because the doc says I'm in A-1 condition, that's why. Nigger, you don't need a better reason than that. Now just haul your black ass back to that jungle and do as you're told. The man doesn't dig Charlie, so *you* shoot some gooks for him and if you get shot doing it, sorry 'bout that shit—maybe we'll give you another medal for it. You're one hell of a lucky nigger to have a second chance to do all this for your country!

Oh, I'm doing some sweet dreaming all right. But I'm not coming up with any good reasons for going back except that if I don't get my ass back in the Nam, it has to be back to America and a Marine prison for at least five years at hard labor and then the rest of my life as an ex-convict. A black ex-convict. There are a hell of a lot of those cats running around America and I don't have to tell you how most of them end up. Some fucking choice: back to Nam and shoot the balls off Charlie, wipe out his families, level his vills—the same old shit for the next six or seven months, if I last that long—or go back home as a goddamn criminal because I won't do Sam's dirty work for him in the Nam.

Do I have the brains and the balls to tell Sam to take his goddamn war and shove it up his big, fucking white ass . . . could I let myself go to prison for doing it, and what the hell would I do with myself when I got out . . . and what the hell do I tell my family I've been doing in Nam for thirteen months? My mother doesn't have a fucking clue; if she ever knew about that kid who picked up my .79 round, oh God, I'd never live in her house again. What happens when my kid brother is old enough to go to Nam. "Knock yourself out, kid, it's just a fuckin' jivetime party." Or do I tell him the truth and have him wondering about what the hell to do with his life and what kind of a motherfucking maniac murderer he has for a big brother?

And if I say *no* to Sam and *no* to America and its jails, then it has to be *no* to everything I know, my family, my block, everybody—have to start out all over again. Either spend the rest of my life on the run or get lucky enough to find someplace where I can live at peace, where the man will never be kicking my black ass into doing his dirty work.

Taki, just how much of a favor were you doing for me when you started asking all those goddamn questions?

Morning. I have to be gone by nine o'clock. It will take at least an hour to get there by cab. If I'm leaving, it has to be soon. That clock is ticking away at the side of the bed and I'm just staring at it. Taki wakes up and looks at the clock. It's getting late. Looks over at me. I'm leaning back, smoking a cigarette. Still Whit, still cool.

She doesn't say a word to me. Her mind must be going a mile a minute, but she is afraid to speak. Taki knows that if she starts in asking more questions, it might provoke me into saying, "Fuck it—I'm going back." I was so goddamn nervous that the smallest provocation, even just a few tears, and I would have blown my top.

Eight thirty. Got up to go to the bathroom. Wash up. Taki had gone back to sleep. Taking my sweet-ass time to shave.

"Terry! Terry! Terry!"

Taki was screaming my name all over the place. She awoke, saw I wasn't in bed and flipped out. Terry's gone!

"What the hell are you screaming about?"

Booom—into the bathroom and all over me. Taki is crying her eyes out.

"I thought you went back. I thought you went back."

"For Christ's sake, stop it! I can't take any more. Just leave me in peace." I sat in bed smoking, watching the clock, looking at Taki. It's now gone nine o'clock.

Fuck you, Sam. Just plain Fuck You, Sam. I lay back on my pillow.

Now it's all over between me and Sam. I had no idea about what the hell I'd do next. Not a clue. I just knew that between me and Sam, the whole fucking crazy game was finished.

Desert? I didn't even know what the fuck the word meant. If anybody had called me a "deserter" then, I'd have kicked his ass. I didn't run away from combat. I did my bit for Sam like a fucking fool. No, definitely no—go back to all that shit in Nam and more of it at home in the States—and for no goddamn good reason? I'm just not that dumb.

It's past ten o'clock. Taki turns over to look at me. A smile of relief on her face. What the hell are you smiling about? I got some rough times ahead of me and you're smiling. Broads. They're all alike.

"Look, Taki, what am I going to do now? Once you mentioned something about going to Kobi."

"Yes, Kobi. Very easy. I get school money from my uncle and we go to Kobi."

Kobi is a big seaport creeping with sailors and slick dicks from every country in the world. They buy and sell everything. Including passports. Taki suggested that I buy a passport and sign on some merchant ship going to a neutral country and live there. Neutral country? Now that sounds pretty good, if there are any. But Kobi is still in Japan. And Japan ain't no neutral country.

There were too many ifs in her plan to try them all out. This is all beginning to piss me off. Have to come up with a good idea soon, because I can't be bullshitting around here much longer. Sam will be looking for me.

"Taki, go find my black buddy. Bring him here. Tell him I have to lie low."

She knew where to find him. At the 45.

"Hey brother, this is it. You made it, man! You got your girl, a pad—what more do you need?"

"I need to get somewhere safer, that's what I need."

"Shit, they give me orders back to Nam and you be damn sure I'm comin' right behind you."

That gave me some encouragement. I'm going to make it. No doubt about it.

After a week of lying low, I decided to step out a bit at night. Scope out the scene. Find out what's happening. At the 45 I ran into a black Pee. SP. Shore Patrol. Nothing to worry about; he was off duty and an old pool-playing buddy of mine from the hospital.

"Hey, brother, I hear you been doing some slippin' around lately?"

"Yeah, I been stepping light. They lookin' for me yet?"

"No. They still think you made it to Nam."

"Well, you be sure to clue in somebody around here as soon as my name comes up."

"Sure thing, brother. You got no sweat."

The coast was clear, so I could do some more checking around town. Hide out during the day. On the prowl at night.

The word had reached all the brothers that Whit was on the run. Everybody had to give his two cents' worth of advice.

"Man, you oughta go to the Russian Embassy."

"The Russian Embassy? You out of your motherfucking mind —what for? I ain't no Communist!"

He had mixed up the story about the Intrepid Four, the first American dudes to split from Japan. According to him, the Russians had helped them to escape.

"The Russians can help you get out of Japan."

"Yeah, right. And live in goddamn Siberia for the rest of my life. You got any more bright ideas?"

They weren't all that dumb. Some of the brothers would bring me food and clothes from the mess halls and PX. So Taki and I weren't hurting too bad. Not yet, anyway.

This outlaw scene lasted about a week or so. Then one night, the Pees ran a check. We were at the 45 when four SP trucks pulled up in front of the club. They were stopping guys on the street for their passes. Pees with guns and clubs and my name. They're after my ass!

The word traveled fast to the back of the bar.

"Whit, they comin' for you."

Oh God, no—why didn't somebody tell me sooner? My blood pressure is sky high. The man got me. If I run, he knows I'm the one he's after. Got to stay cool and still get my ass out of here.

Two plainclothes white cops in coats and ties walk through the door. Obvious as hell in the 45.

Between us and them is a crowd of brothers. They'll have to fight every one of us to get me out of here.

My old buddy was wearing a long white trench coat and a bee-bop cap. He ambled on over to our table. Very casual. Just hanging around. Put the cap on my head. Draped the coat over my shoulders. Dropped some yen in the jukebox. Whispers as he's punching out some sounds.

"Look man, we all gonna dance now. You start dancing your way back to the bathroom."

He brought Taki out on the dance floor. All the brothers stood up to dance. Between the cops and me was every brother in the club. If this doesn't work, nothing will.

"Now, man, now."

Into the bathroom like a shot. A urinal, a commode and a window. What the fuck should I do next?

"Out the window, man."

My buddy was right behind me. Took his coat and hat back, climbed up on the commode and unlocked the window.

"Out you go, brother. Good luck."

"Thanks, man."

I'm scared shitless. The window was high up on the building, so I was able to boost myself up onto the roof. Start moving, baby. No time to be scared of heights. Flying across those China-town roofs, jumping from one to the other. Got to get my ass as far away from the 45 as possible. Came to a wide street. Too wide to jump.

There was a mechanic's shop down below where a couple of Japanese were working on a car. They spotted me leaning over the roof. Where the hell did this nut come from?

A wooden gate was next to the building. Slid down it and split for the corner. The Japanese cats didn't say a word. Just watched. They must have figured out what was happening.

Hit the corner. Goddamn, I thought I was out of sight of the 45 by now! There it was about a mere one hundred yards from me. Shit. The Pees were still out in front of the place. Stay cool, babe. Just walk nice and slow in the opposite direction and hop in the first cab that comes along.

My mind was running so fast, I stopped at the corner and waited for the light to change. Don't get nailed breaking any laws right now. The light was green—for me. And I'm standing there like a damn fool waiting for it to change!

An SP truck pulls up at the red light. The goddamn Pees! Right in front of me. Nowhere to go now. Just waiting for the word. Hands up, motherfucker, we got you now.

The dude at the window nodded hello. Yeah, hello yourself, for Christ's sake. Stop looking at me, you goddamn idiot!

The light changed and the Pees drove off. A red light. I still have to wait. O sweet pleadin' Jesus, send me a motherfucking taxi now!

There he goes—hop right in.

"Atsugi. Atsugi."

Atsugi is the goddamn base, but it's the only place in town from which I can direct a cab to Taki's street. I can't even pronounce the street's name.

"Move, man, move."

Another crazy, drunken GI to bring home. That's what he's thinking.

It didn't take more than a few minutes to get to the base; I have to flag him down and around to the right before he hits that gate!

"Go right, man, *right!*"

He's shaking his head no and aiming for the gate. Doesn't understand a word I'm saying.

"Atsugi. Atsugi."

And he's pointing at the gate. Shit, I know it's Atsugi base, but I sure as hell don't want him to go there. Whack him on his right shoulder and point like mad in the same direction. Just in time. Sharp turn to the right and we're off. Whew! I could see that jarhead's spit-polished boots shining, we passed so close.

Straight ride across town and we'll be at Taki's house. Look in my pocket for some yen to pay the man. No yen. That's O.K., Taki always has some money around the house. Look in my other pocket for the key. Taki had it!

No, it's all over now, babe. This man is bound to call the cops and they sure as hell will hand me over to the Pees. Taki, if you ain't home, it's the brig for me. Please, dear God, may she be home!

There isn't a light on in the house. She's still out. Climb in a goddamn window, that's all. Now this cabdriver will surely think I'm bolting if I leave his cab without producing some yen. He doesn't understand a word of English, so there's no use in giving him a song and dance routine.

"Hold this. Hold this."

If I give him my billfold with no money in it, just my military ID, maybe he'll get the idea. "Crazy drunk GI" look from him. But he doesn't stop me.

Walked slowly to the side of the house and then ran like hell —*thud!* Knocked somebody right on his ass. Oh God, what next, now will they get me for assault too? It was Taki.

"Pay that man, goddamnit. Pay him."

In the house, crawl up in a corner, light a cigarette and drink my green tea. Wheeeew! Please, no more games like that one.

I must have smoked two packs of cigarettes that night while peeping out the window for the man. No sleep.

A chief petty officer lived directly across the street from Taki. I don't know where he worked or if he knew that I had split, but he scared the shit out of me sitting right across the street. We'd even exchange hellos in the morning as he was going to work and I'd be picking up the paper or carrying out the garbage. Me in my little kimono. Brass balls Whit!

They'd soon be on to Taki, so I knew that I'd have to be splitting.

"Taki, get my black buddy up here fast."

He clued me in on what had happened that night at the 45. The Pees had seen me go into the bathroom and pushed their way through the crowd after me. Too late. I was gone. They stayed around to question people, got nowhere and left. My buddy was certain that they were suspicious of Taki. That does it. It's only a matter of time and they got me in irons. If I can't find a way out of here, it would be easier on me if I surrendered.

"Surrender? You out of your motherfucking mind? They'll send you straight back to Nam, set you on point and some goddamn hillbilly lifer'll put a bullet in your back. Then you ain't goin' nowhere no more."

"What about a priest? You go talk to a chaplain and maybe we can make a deal through you."

"You're crazy. No military priest will fall for that shit. They'll zap you."

"I gotta do something."

"O.K. I'll try to talk to a priest for you."

Two days and nights passed with me holed up in Taki's house, waiting for a word from the priest. Nothing.

"Taki, go look for him at the 45. If something has happened, I have to know about it fast."

She slipped around town to scope out the news. It was none too good.

The brother had received his orders home the day after he left me. He was stateside and I was dicked! But that wasn't half of it. Even my white buddy wasn't around to help me any longer. Although he had been badly shot in the arm, it was a small flesh wound in his leg that had kept him in Japan so long. Each time he took a leak, he dabbed a little piss on his leg wound to keep it infected. The doctors couldn't figure out why it wasn't getting better. So he stayed in Japan. This went on for several months until gangrene spread through his whole leg and they cut it off. Now he was heading home—the hard way.

So I'm all alone. Just me and Taki and every Pee in Yokohama hunting after my ass. Then along came Paul. My Japanese brother to the rescue.

Paul had come up with some screwy ideas in the past. I had been worried about the Pees searching my locker at the base and finding pictures of Taki and me, and of course ol' Lynchin' Baines Johnson. Paul offered to sneak in and get them for me.

"Paul, if they see your Japanese face anywhere near those barracks, they'll shoot your ass off. They got trigger-happy young boots on those gates and they're all wearing loaded .45s."

Crazy, good-hearted Paul. He'd have died for me if I didn't stop him. But it was Paul who came up with my one way ticket out of Japan.

Bang . . . bang . . . bang! In the middle of the night, they're rapping on the windows. Fuck, they found me! Ran behind the door. Maybe Taki could bullshit them out of coming in. She swallowed hard and opened the door. It was only Paul. Mad fool was only making sure we'd wake up.

"Paul, I almost killed you. I still feel like breaking your goddamn neck."

"No, no. You want to leave Japan? You want to be safe?"

"What the fuck do you think? Now slow down and tell me what the hell it's all about."

"Here, here. They help you."

He handed me card, Japanese writing all over it.

"Taki, translate this shit."

She read it and her mouth swung open. Ran to her desk and tore through some magazines.

"Look, Terry. They left. They help you."

"Who left where? What the hell you talkin' about?"

She showed me a picture of Rick Bailey and the rest of the Intrepid Four. I didn't know who they were then.

"They leave Japan and go to Sweden. Live in Sweden."

Sweden? I knew as much about Sweden as I did about Ant-
arctica.

"Tell me more."

"These people on card. They help you leave Japan."

"What people?"

"Beheiren."

BEHEIREN

"Call 'em, Taki. Go out and call those people now."

We called from a public phone booth in case Beheiren's phone was tapped and calls were traced. My first time playing with the international undergound, I was one very frightened cat. Deserting. That was supposed to have been a hell of a serious crime according to the military. I'd been gone all this time but never really thought about it, never considered myself a deserter. Deserters? Those are guys who turn and run in combat, split for the rear where it's safe. Well, not quite. The military sees them as anybody who has split for more than thirty days from anywhere at anytime. Now that makes for one hell of a lot of deserters from the American military. One every few minutes according to the latest statistics.

"Beheiren helps deserters to escape from Japan. Help you to a neutral country."

Well, they can help me become one of those statistics. Goddamn, if only ol' Lynchin' Baines Johnson could see me now!

Taki spoke to the Beheiren people on the phone. They're rapping Japanese a mile a minute, while I'm eyeballing every passing car.

"We have to meet them tomorrow in Yokohama center."

"That's a big place, right out in public. I hope these dudes know what they're doing."

Paul and Taki came with me to translate and maybe run a little interference if the going got rough. Our cab pulled up to a tall office building—headquarters for all kinds of Japanese newspapers.

Taki showed the card to the receptionist, who didn't know what the hell it was all about. Don't push it; we'd better slip on out before she starts asking questions.

"Can I help you?"

In English. Some Japanese dude had walked up behind us. He spotted me as a black American and put two and two together.

"I bring you to Beheiren. Please follow me quickly."

We walked upstairs into a large room packed with newsmen pounding away on their typewriters. Hell, I ain't giving no press conference now! This is supposed to be secret and they're going to be blabbing it all over Japan. . . . I'm leaving before they fuck me up good.

"No, no. No story. We only meet here. I'm not from the organization, but we say nothing. We just put you in contact with the organization. You sure you know what you do?"

"Yep."

After a short wait, a slippery dude came sliding in the door. Black beret down over his head, long, baggy old overcoat, unshaved—the exact opposite of all the snappy-looking newsmen.

"I am representative from Beheiren. We cannot talk here. Go someplace else."

Out of the office and head for the elevators.

"No. Must take back way. This building is watched."

Watched? And we haven't been caught yet! Whew.

"The police know we sometimes operate here."

Down the stairway, into the cellar, out the back door. Another scudzy dude waiting with a car. He mumbles something to Taki and she gets ready to bug out.

"Wait a minute. You don't go nowhere. I want to know every word these dudes are saying and what they're doing."

"But it is very dangerous for her."

"It's gonna be a lot more dangerous if she ain't along. Where I go, she goes."

Zoom—zoom, around the block about three times and down some side street.

"When I get out, you get out."

Screeech. Pulls up right next to a cab . . . doors fly open . . . out of the car and into the cab. He doesn't have to say a word to the cabdriver, who seems to know exactly where he's going.

Zoom—zoom. Follow me again. *Screeech.* He's out and running towards another cab. But this one is across the street and headed in the opposite direction. Confusion. He makes it, but we have to wait for the traffic. All these goddamn little Toyotas and I just know that one of them has my name written on it. He's waving his hands for us to run across.

We're off again in another cab. Now this is a gas. I'm not scared anymore; it's getting to be fun watching these Beheiren dudes operate. In and out of waiting cabs, never even paying a bill.

We changed cars and cabs several more times and ended up far outside of town at a construction site. Our little gang gathered in a temporary office. Now what? This dude is staring at his watch, peeping out the window. Taki and I are munching on some sandwiches he gave us.

"You O.K.? You comfortable?"

"Yeah, I'm all right. But what about you? You're the one who's got the jitters."

"We must wait."

Fine by me, but I'd sure as hell like to know where we are just in case something happens and I have to punch out a few dudes. If Taki and I have to make a run for it, it'd be nice to know how to get out of here. But she hasn't a clue about where we are.

In walks a bearded cat.

"Now we shall go. This place not too safe."

Isn't any place safe around here? And for weeks I've been walking around the streets at night. God, you just keep right on taking good care of Whit.

This time we take a more ordinary form of transportation—a bus. Nice quiet ride through the countryside until we pull up to a stop before a river. We pile out and into a waiting car. These Beheiren cats are about the slickest operators since Al Capone and his boys.

We followed the river to a large hotel. Never a word from them except "Are you comfortable? Are you scared?"

If I'm scared, they won't know it. Whit must be cool.

"When we check into the hotel, you must use this name and identification."

I'm supposed to be an East African living and studying in England. If any East African cat starts rapping to me in Swahili, I'm lost. So the idea is for me to keep my mouth shut as much as possible. A hard job, but I'll try.

Each time we switched places and rooms, the Beheiren people changed. Each one chatted with me, just curious. None of them ever laid on a political or anti-American rap, which slightly surprised me. Why the hell are they helping me anyway? But no time to ask questions. We're off for another car ride. This time to a Beheiren hideout for a conference.

The organization had a lot of members present for a big rap with me.

"Do you really know what you are doing and how very dangerous it is for you."

"Yep."

"We want you to know that we're not absolutely sure we can help you. We only *try* to help you get away from war. We are all pacifists and try very hard to help men who do not want to kill. We have helped other Americans, so maybe we can help you too. But we cannot guarantee you freedom in another country."

"Well, if you're trying, I'll try with you."

"We are not a marriage bureau. If someone deserts just for a girl, we do not help him. You must understand what you are doing and be very serious."

"I can't get no more serious than I am."

The first thing I clued them in on was how many years Sam could lay me up in the brig. Sam isn't about to allow a black Man's conscience as an excuse for not doing as he's told. The Man just doesn't dig any wise-mouth back talk. Then it really hit home to me, and I let them know it, that not only was I refusing to kill or be killed in Nam, but I was refusing to be a part of that country which was fucking over my own people. I said "that" country, not "my" country. It never belonged to me or my people and never would. The only things back there which were a part of me were my family, my block and the daughter I'd never seen. My family I'd miss like hell, but they'd never completely understand what I did; maybe my old man could figure it out, but not the others. They'd miss me too of course, but they could make it without me. My block—I'd be too old for it when I returned and too goddamn hard-assed to be playing around with kids after spending time in prison and months in the Nam shooting at kids. But my daughter—she was my only regret, my only worry about never being able to return to the States. No, I couldn't go back to killing kids in Nam—I told Beheiren that. And no, I could never go back to being a piss-poor black ex-con in Memphis with a shot-up ass and the finger from Sam. I told the Japanese plenty of good reasons for saying, "Fuck you, Sam"—but I couldn't bring myself to tell them a word about my daughter. It wasn't until I had reached Sweden and the news had hit the Memphis papers, that I received a letter from my mother which finally put my mind a little at ease. She had my daughter. She would raise her. Her own mother would have nothing more to do with me now that I was no longer a big, bad Marine war hero. I was just another one of those motherfucking, faggot, Commie deserters.

"So you will never go back to America either?"

"Nope, never."

Not go back to Nam—that wasn't so hard. I didn't have to spend weeks thinking about that one—Con Thien, my ass shot up for nothing—that was just a question of whether I was dumb enough or crazy enough to go back to Nam. Good little black boy that I was, I almost went back. The man says Go, I go. Kill, I kill. Die, I die. If it hadn't been for all those delays, I would never even have had the time to think beforehand. But Taki said think, and I thought, probably for the first time in my life. And the answer was very fucking obvious: It's your war,

Sam, you fight it. Nam is no place for an American, much less a black man.

But the States—no matter how bad it was for my people there, no matter how many good reasons I could come up with for not going back to America, it still hurt. But if Nam has to be out, the same goes for America. If I'm not dumb enough to go back to Nam, I can't be dumb enough to go to prison for *not* killing people. No college degree, but I'm no fucking moron either.

If America is out and Japan isn't safe . . . where? What country will take a black American deserter—refugee—immigrant or whatever the hell you want to call me? If it's not a Communist country—and I hoped to God it wouldn't be—then it will have to be a country with very big balls, because Sam is sure to bring beaucoup smoke on that country's ass.

The Beheiren dudes just listened. They didn't encourage me or pat me on the back. It was my decision to make and they realized that. They knew that I must have a lot of good reasons to split, but they wanted to be certain that I was convinced that they were good reasons and that I wasn't fooling myself about what lay ahead of me.

They were making sure that I wasn't a bullshitter, a wise-ass kid or just too stupid to understand what I was doing. After I convinced them that it wasn't just a dumb stunt, they still insisted on giving me more time to think about it.

"You go back to hotel. Tomorrow you go home. Taki knows where to contact us when you are ready to go."

At night, I tried to put all the pieces together.

"Taki, just what can these guys do for me?"

"They take you on boat to Russia. Then you go to country where you can stay and be free. Some go to Sweden, some to Cuba. But you must take trip alone. I cannot go."

She was pissed. Taki wanted to come along, but they had laid the word down.

"You leave?" she asked.

"Of course. I have to."

"You leave Taki. Why? Stay with me. You go to Sweden. I know what Swedish girls are like. They all want to sleep with men all the time. You never see me again."

"I'll send for you. Goddamnit, you know I have to leave Japan and it's got to be by myself."

"No help. I give no help. Go. Go now."

I have to travel to Tokyo to meet the big man from Beheiren. It's an hour's ride on the train and then a hunt for the restaurant near the Tokyo Central Station where we're supposed to meet. Taki must come along to guide me.

"Taki, are you coming with me to Tokyo? I can't find the way by myself. How am I going to ask directions in Japanese? I don't want to arouse suspicion."

"You can't go by yourself. That's why I don't go."

Stubborn bitch. She starts to get dressed.

"Where you going?"

"Shopping."

"Look, we gotta call a cab and split soon. Stop acting like a baby."

To hell with you. With or without her, I'm making it. She went out the door ahead of me, walking about twenty feet in front of me in the direction of the corner. The street ends in a small roundabout. I've got my hands stuffed in my pockets, pissed, scared but determined to make it.

The Pees! An SP jeep cruises right up behind me and towards the roundabout. Keep cool. Keep your head down, Whit. And Taki, for Christ's sake, don't react.

"Terry! Oh, Terry!"

As the jeep turns around, she turns to warn me. Like I'm blind and can't see the jeep. Dumb broad! Keep walking. Shut your goddamn mouth and keep walking.

The Pees creep right by me at ten miles per hour. Not even a sign of recognition. Whew! Got to leave this neighborhood fast. Too many of these bastards live around here and their buddies are always cruising by to give them a lift to work.

"Terry, I'm so scared for you."

"If you're so damn scared, just shut your mouth and take me to Tokyo."

She called a cab and we were off. Down to the train station and off for Tokyo.

On a crowded train, everyone is Japanese but me—a six-foot black man arguing with one of their pretty little girls.

"You made me do this. I should have let them take you."

"Shut up, for Christ's sake! You got everybody staring at us."

She knows the older Japanese men in the car probably resent her being with a foreigner. So to spite them, she throws her arms around me to attract even more attention! Just what I need.

"Taki, ain't you got no sense? Behave yourself, before you get me killed."

Tokyo Central Station was like a giant anthill. Never in all my life have I seen so many people running around one place. And every white man I saw, I could have sworn he was CIA, CID, FBI, SP, MP, AP . . . some bastard just out looking for me.

The meeting place was an exclusive restaurant near the station. Rendezvous at noon. Take a seat in the corner. Order some beers and ham sandwiches. Twelve thirty. No show. This cat is supposed to know me. We've met before. The jitters set in.

"You see him, Taki? You see him?"

"No. No."

One o'clock. One thirty.

"You sure he said noon?"

A young Japanese reading a book at the table in front of us pipes up.

"Terry? I am a representative from Beheiren."

"Goddamn, you've been sitting right across from us for almost two hours. Why didn't you say something?"

"We must be sure. This place is not too safe. I pay check. You follow me."

Not safe? Here we go again.

He led us through underground tunnels to a cab. Drove to

his parents' house, where he had a pad on the ground floor. He and Taki started to jabber.

"They can't take me with you. Terry, I have to leave now."

"Now? Why?"

"We must be very cautious. Your girl must leave."

"O.K."

Good-bye kisses and tears. This is it. On my own now. These Beheiren boys had better know their stuff.

After dinner we were on the road again. To a big-time journalist's house. He had been banned from entering the U.S. because he had once been stationed in Peking as a foreign correspondent. I don't see why that's grounds for keeping him out of the States, but in the past few months I'd been learning all kinds of new things about Sam. There's no telling just what Sam may try to pull next. Nothing would surprise me.

This journalist was on his way to Czechoslovakia in a few days. Not to write any stories but to open up a new route for Beheiren. The Soviet Union was getting a little sticky, I guess. Czechoslovakia seemed like a better deal then, in the spring of 1968. Still not a word about where I'd eventually be going.

Staying in all these different Japanese homes, I had to get used to eating strictly Japanese food. Good food, and free, so I couldn't complain in any case. Breakfast was usually an absolutely tasteless block of white jelly. If I have to eat, I have to eat. My host put some soya on his whatever-it-was. I tried the same. Delicious! Not ham and eggs, but good-tasting nonetheless.

The two Capone boys from my first day's adventure with Beheiren came by to take me for a train ride after breakfast.

"Where we going?"

"Take a little trip."

And we commenced to ride on a blue, stream-lined special to God-knows-where.

"We keep you in countryside, away from Tokyo. You are guest of Dr. Igawi."

An old gentleman with white hair and a constant smile. He

and his wife lived way up in the hills, where he was a country doctor and preacher.

"We glad to have you here. You eat now."

And his wife took off for the cellar to find a knife and fork for me.

"I know we have some, but I cannot find them."

"That's O.K. You teach me to use chopsticks."

Groovy. Lots of food. My own room. Watching TV with the family. In the mornings we'd collect eggs from his chicken farm. He'd make his doctor's rounds and then we'd do some fishing in the afternoons. The mountain streams were jumping with all kinds of good eating fish.

And we'd rap. About Vietnam, about my health. With all that walking in the hills, my legs had begun to give me a lot of pain. Dr. Igawi examined me.

"You were hurt very badly and still are not completely well. War is a terrible thing. No real human should be forced to do such things."

He knew what he was talking about. His left arm had been torn up badly by a grenade back in the "big war." So I wasn't the only warrior in that tiny village.

"You take these pills while you're here. They kill the pain."

Sunday was church day. The doctor gave a sermon in Japanese, of course. I didn't understand a word of it nor any of the hymns, but it reminded me of home. Of my family, whom I might never see again. Got to put thoughts like these out of my mind.

It was a Protestant church, so some of the songs were familiar to me. When they sang "Michael Row the Boat Ashore" in Japanese, I joined in with the English lyrics. And on the Hallelujahs, we were all together.

After six days with Dr. Igawi and his wife, I felt like their son. Momma-san was already teaching me Japanese. Then I got a call one night.

"Someone wants to talk to you, Terry."

It's Taki.

"I miss you, I want to see you."

She's whining away and I'm getting horny as hell.

"They want to speak to Dr. Igawi now," she said.

He got on the phone and his face became very sad.

"Terry, they say you must go tonight. I tell them it's O.K. up here, but they say you must move."

If they say so, I have to. We all knew that, but it was a sad departure. Momma-san had red eyes when she said good-bye to me. What could I say to these lovely people except "Thank you, you've been very kind to me"?

Beheiren came to pick me up that same night.

Back towards a suburb of Tokyo. I don't know which one, but when we reached it, the car left us at a train station. We rode the train only two stops and then walked for a few blocks.

Clop-clop . . . clop-clop . . . clop—clop. Somebody's running up behind us. *Whoom*—he's on my back! I'll kill the motherfucker before I'll let them take me in!

Taki. That crazy broad. Beheiren had smuggled her out to see me. They even arranged a little love nest for us. She must have pestered the Beheiren people morning, noon and night for them to go through all this trouble.

We were to be the guests of a lady professor from the University of Tokyo who had taught at Princeton. Her library was enormous with one whole shelf filled only with books she had written.

"What'll you have?"

"Uhh?" What's this? I was used to Japanese customs and green tea. This chick from Princeton pops up with "What'll you have?"

"Scotch, gin, an aperitif?"

"Unh, I don't drink, but if you have Coke, I'd like one."

She gave me a shit-eating grin.

"Well, *maybe* I have one hidden away especially for guests."

The boys from Beheiren had a good laugh. It seems that all

these people tried to avoid buying American products whenever they could. And Coke is about as American as they come.

She gave me a Coke and I drank it. Unashamed. I was too thirsty.

Taki was unable to stay for the entire night. After a few hours, some representatives from Beheiren arrived to take her home. Before going to bed, I rapped for a while with the professor. One of the Intrepid Four had stayed with her during the winter, so she was not new at making nervous young Americans feel right at home.

"What would you like for breakfast?"

"Anything. Whatever you're having is fine with me."

She left a note for the maid with my breakfast instructions. She was off to teach an early class by the time I came down. Breakfast was waiting for me. Ham and eggs! Cold milk, toast and jam. The professor was a perfect hostess. She even went so far as to invite Taki back to spend the night.

Taki showed up with an enormous cake. Here in Sweden, we usually bring flowers when we visit someone. In Japan, they bring cakes or cookies. We all knocked ourselves out on that cake. And then settled down for the night. Lovely!

By morning it was time for me to move again. Seeing Taki was becoming a habit, so neither one of us felt too sad when we kissed good-bye. It was to be the last time I'd see her.

Beheiren drove me to another priest's house in the suburbs. He was a very busy man who didn't speak English well. One of the younger Beheiren representatives stayed there to keep me company. We played cards, bullshitted, watched Japanese baseball on TV and cooked our food together. He prepared the Japanese dishes while I cooked the American. Between the two of us we usually managed to burn everything.

From the priest's church across the street, I could hear the hymn-singing. It was too dangerous for me to leave the house, even to go to church. And I wanted so badly to be singing with them. Being trapped like this, feeling like a real fugitive for the first time, I became depressed. The thought of going home and

even of turning myself in had entered my mind. But not for
long.

One night, the young dude and I stayed upstairs to rap while
the family watched TV. We were swapping stories about the
neighborhoods we grew up in—my block in Memphis, his in
Hamamatsu. Of course I told him how great my block was, what
a groovy town Memphis was. Never mentioned that the block
was in a ghetto. I grooved on all this sentimental shit as much
as he did. We were having a fine time swapping stories.

"Terry! Terry! Come quick. King dead. King dead!"

The little old priest came busting into the room, shouting
away. What the hell is he talking about?

"Look TV. Shoot King! Shoot King!"

What king is he talking about? The Japanese still have a king?
I hop on downstairs in my little kimono. The whole family is
gathered around the TV set. On the screen are a lot of buildings.
It's America, but I don't recognize the city itself until the name
flashes across the side of the screen: Memphis!

"Martin Luther King is dead. He was shot in Memphis, Tennessee, while standing on the balcony of his room at the
Motel . . ."

That King! Martin Luther King murdered in my home town
. . . in Memphis . . . the rotten motherfuckers! Go back? To
what? To all that shit . . . to those goddamn barbarians who
can't stop killing people wherever they go? Fuck you, Sam . . .
fuck you and all your crazy followers with you!

I had just finished telling this dude how nice Memphis was.
Thoughts about my family were lingering in my mind . . .
thoughts about going back. How dumb can you get, Whit? No,
that does it. Never. Never will I return to that insane asylum
America!

Whatever doubts I might have had in my mind just poured
themselves out of me that night. They were gone and I was
straight about what I had to do. Where I was going was still un-

certain. I was only determined that I'd never return to the States.

"Terry, we may have to send you to Cuba."

Beheiren was finally giving me an inkling of what might happen.

"But it will be a very dangerous trip. You must take a boat through the Panama Canal."

That's nice. It's sunny and warm down there. What's the big problem?

"The Americans make a very careful inspection of every boat passing through the Canal."

That's the big problem—an inspection by the American military. Hell, they even have a big Green Beret training center in the Canal Zone. No, the tropical cruise had suddenly lost its appeal.

"But we are not sure about this trip. If necessary, would you be willing to live in the Cuban Embassy for some time while we arrange your escape? There is another American living there now."

Then he told me the story about Kim, a Korean-American who had refused to return to Nam, spent some time in a military stockade and then escaped into the underground. Beheiren had set him up at the Cuban Embassy. Well, if I had to go there, at least I'd have some company.

The Beheiren representative discussed several other plans, all of them just suggestions. I think that they were testing my sincerity again, because nothing was decided then in spite of all the discussion about escape routes.

After this meeting, I thought that the Cuban Embassy would probably be my home for a while. Two days later a car pulled up for me.

"We must leave quickly. Your friend Paul has been arrested."

The story was that Paul had been beaten up badly in a fight with some GIs. When the police came, they found his pistol, which he had recently begun to carry for protection. From what,

I don't know. It was a stupid thing for him to have done, because now he was in the custody of the Japanese police. Beheiren was afraid that he might be tempted to swap some of the information he knew about the organization and me in exchange for his own release. If he spilled what he knew, several people would be facing very stiff prison sentences. Beheiren was not about to take any chances with Paul.

"It is time for us to take you out of Japan. It is probable that you'll be meeting another American very soon."

That afternoon, in slinked Joe Kametz. Joe was to be my sidekick for the next few months. But at that first meeting, he was only the first white American with whom I had had close contact in several weeks. We were both very uptight. Cautiously eyeballing each other over before saying a word.

"Hi, what's your name?"

"Terry."

"Joe."

Then we traded tales. Joe was a rough motherfucker, also a Marine. He'd told them several times that he wouldn't return to Nam or go to the brig for it. They replied by throwing him in an isolation cell. He sat in the dark for a month straight. Couldn't stand up. Only stale bread, water and a half-head of lettuce to eat every day. An open hole in the floor for a shitter, which only the guard could flush—when he felt like it.

"Yeah, I was a pretty quiet dude when I got out. Didn't give them no more trouble."

Joe had no intention to return to Nam. He just wasn't about to shoot his mouth off and rub their noses in it anymore.

A third American joined us that night. A crazy Army dude, Pappy Arnett, about thirty-five years old, skinny, slow and still an E-4 cook in the Army. A sorry, sorry individual. He should have never been allowed into the military. Too retarded even for the Army. As a matter of fact, they didn't let him in for years. It wasn't until McNamara let in his 100,000-plus retarded whiz kids that Pappy was allowed to enlist. The Army was really hurting for men as Nam dragged on and on.

How old Pappy made it to Beheiren, I'll never figure out. He must have approached someone while on R and R in Japan. In his case, Beheiren was putting pity before common sense. As it turned out, he didn't last long as an exile. The immigrant life was too much for him. He gave himself up to the American Embassy in Stockholm several months after arriving in Sweden. Just the kind of nut they love to get. Rewarded him with four years' hard labor at Leavenworth and a dishonorable discharge, even though his lawyer had Army psychiatrists testifying that he was too retarded even to be one of the Army's boys.

That makes three of us.

"You gentlemen will soon be taking a trip through the Soviet Union. The trip will begin with a plane ride to the north of Japan. Then you will travel by boat to the Soviet Union."

Russia! What happened to Cuba? None of us were too keen on going to Russia, but we didn't have much choice at this stage of the game. And if we meet some Russians who are as good-hearted as these Beheiren people, we won't have too much to worry about. That is, the other guys won't have too much to worry about. They're white and so are the Russians. I was a little chickenshit about going to a country where there were only white people.

"You will be meeting some more Americans in the morning."

This is it. We'll be gone from Japan in a day or two. And then God only knows what in Siberia. *Brrrrr!* Just the thought of Russia gave me the shakes.

And Taki? Will I get a chance to say good-bye to her?

"Too dangerous. You give us letter. We mail it after you leave. You leave soon. If anyone does not want to go on this trip, he can wait in Japan. Maybe we get him out later."

Maybe? If we're going, we might as well get it over with now. Split while we know there's at least a chance of making it. This underground fugitive shit is no way to spend a lifetime.

"If you are ready, we take you to airport in morning. There will be many students at airport tomorrow who will have big demonstration. If there is any trouble, they have instructions to create chaos. As military men, you should know how to take care of yourselves after that."

Some more of that Al Capone stuff again. I'm really going to miss these Beheiren boys.

We all slipped into the air terminal separately. Shades on, collars up, hanging around in the corners, we were playing it carefully. The idea was to avoid attention and keep an eye out for the other Americans who were supposed to come with us. They were already upstairs doing the same thing. We just about ran over each other.

Phil Callico came down first. Navy, about nineteen years old but looking younger, he swaggered like a goddamn colonel. Tough guy.

Mark Shapiro—Joe College in the flesh. Scruffy beard, eye-glasses, tennis shoes, sport coat and a scared-shitless look on his face. Lugging a huge suitcase with both hands. God only knows what could be so valuable that he has to carry it with him at a time like this.

Our gang has gathered. What a collection! Jumpy as cats, we're the last ones to get on line for the plane to Hokkaido. I guess we weren't as obvious as we felt, but it seemed awfully hard to be completely anonymous. A woman was collecting our tickets when the commotion started. Dumb fucking Shapiro—he still has his goddamn suitcase and he's trying to get on the plane with it!

"Let's go, man. Throw the motherfucker away!"

The stewardess wouldn't let him through the gate with such a big piece of luggage.

"No, I can't throw it away. I need it."

"Dumb fuck, then stay here with it, 'cause we're leaving."

The whole damn airport must be staring at us by now. After all that shouting at Mark with his suitcase, somebody took pity on him at the last minute and packed his suitcase in the back of the plane. Run for it. Five deserters from the American military running across the field to catch a plane for Hokkaido. What a sight!

Sit back. Relax. It's good-bye Tokyo. Freedom soon! What a groovy feeling as that plane took off. Time to breathe easy and get some sleep.

Ow! Some nut is beating on my shoulder . . . cops! They're waking me up. They got us where it counts. Right in the act. Nope, just some dopy lady tourist next to me who wanted to be sure I didn't sleep through all the sights. Can't miss those beautiful mountaintops.

"Yeah, they're lovely, but I really need my sleep. Thanks anyway."

I'd like to bounce you off those mountaintops.

Hokkaido. We're supposed to be big-time American tourists who like to keep to ourselves, with our own car and chauffeur, no less.

"Are you Americans up here for the day?" A restaurant owner figured us to be some very loaded cats. "I also have nightclub with girls downtown. You come?"

Callico and Shapiro—the dumb kids—encourage the dude.

"Yeah, sure we'll be there. Thanks a lot."

"Shut up, turds. We ain't supposed to be attracting attention."

Even the Japanese woman who had come with us from Beheiren had to keep her mouth shut. She spoke Japanese with a strong southern accent, which would have caused the people on Hokkaido to wonder why an out-of-towner was guiding tourists on their island.

She got us off the streets in a hurry and set us up in a fishing-boat-captain's house. He welcomed us all with a bottle of saki. Joe loved the juice, so he went right to it.

"Tonight you will be my guests."

"We gonna sleep here?"

"No. I'm going to take you in my boat to meet the Soviet Coast Guard."

What the fuck? Now we're all ears and very scared. Joe just about finished the bottle of saki.

"You must trust me. I hate war too. I was kamikaze pilot in war. I come back. You trust me."

Ain't no choice. The skipper fitted us out with Japanese fishermen's outfits. At night we were going to walk down to his boat before the crew arrived. They wouldn't know about us.

It was a very cold night. No clouds but no moon either. The dock was lit with floodlights, so I had to roll a blanket around my shoulders as a hood. With their heads low and walking fast, the other dudes might pass for Japanese. But not me. Beheiren wasn't taking any chances with my black skin.

So we're off to meet the Russian Coast Guard. Ooowee! That gave me the shivers. Nobody had told us what was up after that. We'd rendezvous at sea with the Russians. That's all we knew.

The captain led us down to a space below his cabin. Dark, wet and very cold. These fishermen's outfits were too thin for any protection. Thank God for my little blanket.

"Freedom, baby, freedom! We gonna be free!"

Joe was grooving out loud. The captain had told us to be quiet, but Joe couldn't hold it in. Also, he had drunk too much saki to keep his mouth shut. Yet he was only expressing what each one of us felt but were too scared to say.

Somebody's coming! The door opened, quick crack of light and *boom,* the door slams. Somebody else is standing in the dark with us.

"Kim? Kim?"

Joe had heard that a yellow-skinned cat might join us, so he figured it might be the Korean-American who had been living at the Cuban Embassy.

"Yeah, it's me."

We're all together now. Six fugitives from America literally in the same boat—a smelly old heap. The crew came aboard quickly and we shoved off. Uuusch—seasick. The sea was rough right from the start. Goddamn, don't make any noise puking because the crew isn't supposed to know we're down here. Joe is the only one not bothered by a thing. He has another bottle of saki and is too stoned to be feeling any pain.

"Gimme a swig."

Usually I don't drink, but this was a special occasion. I needed something. Those waves were high and we were bouncing hard. Kim puked. What a stink.

"Blow it out, baby. Let it all hang out. We gonna be free soon."

Joe was too much. He kept it up for hours. The ship was out there rolling around on those waves for a hell of a long time. We could barely see out the porthole, but Joe swore that he was seeing dolphins and helicopters. Not a damned thing but waves out there.

And then a bright light. A searchlight! Scramble over each other to get a good look through the porthole.

"It's them, man. The Russians are coming! We gonna be free now, baby. Fuck you, Sam!"

RUSSIAN HOSPITALITY

A powerful searchlight was all we could see of the Soviet Coast Guard ship. It took a long time for it to come side by side with us. The sea was rocking the hell out of both ships, so it was a tough job to hitch them together. As one rose on a wave, the other sank.

"It's gonna be a bitch to jump across those waves."

A Russian started to give orders in Japanese to the fishing crew. They were running every which way, opening hatches, throwing lines. The excuse for all this was supposed to be an inspection of the fishing catch by a Russian officer. He leaped down to the fishing boat's deck and the Japanese crew followed him below for a look at the fish. This is our cue. The skipper opened the door and gave us the go sign—run for it!

Boom—Kim is out like a flash—around the smokestack, climb the railing. The Russian ship slid down a wave. Kim jumped when the two were even, landing on the Russian deck as it went below the level of the fishing boat. He didn't waste any time.

I held the door open for the other guys. Joe was next. All that saki didn't slow him down a bit.

"Free now, babe. We're free, really free!"

Whooom—about a five- or six-foot leap and he was safe, laughing his fool head off.

Phil damn near slipped off the boat as he slid around the smokestack into a leaping position. There was no railing in front of the smokestack and both the deck and stack were soaking wet. Jumping like a Tarzan, he made it.

"I can't do it! I can't go around that. Isn't there another way?"

Fucking Mark—Joe College cry baby won't slide around the smokestack.

"Leave the pussy behind, Whit! You jump."

Joe didn't give a shit about anybody who might screw his chances for freedom.

"Jump, you dumb cunt, jump!"

Legs and arms flying, Mark made it.

Pappy was slow as shit. Fuck you, I'm not waiting all night. Slide . . . wait for the boats to get level . . . *whooosh*—I'm over!

Hello, Ivan! Landed right in the arms of two huge Russian bears. Huge? These bastards were about six feet six, giants covered in fur hats and fur coats. They caught me in midair and set me down. Glad you guys are on my side this time.

Pappy was up on deck. He made it around the smokestack and perched for his leap. The asshole waited until the Russian ship was on the rise, instead of on the descent.

Whooosh—whack! Only one leg made it over the railing. The other leg, with Pappy attached to it, was dangling above the waves. A Russian held his leg, while I stretched over the side and pulled him up by his arm.

"My leg is bleeding. I think it's broke!"

"Your own goddamn fault. Pappy, you are one stupid motherfucker."

Then it was Mark's turn to cry again.

"My suitcase! My suitcase is still over there!"

What the hell does he have in that goddamn thing—gold? We had to wait for Mark's fucking suitcase again. The captain went below, dragged it up and heaved it across.

"Mark, if we have any more trouble with your fucking suitcase, it goes over and you with it!"

Well, here we are on a Communist ship, cannons and all. We were free, all right, but I wasn't too wild about those big Russian bears and their cannons.

We were led down into the ship and showed to our rooms in the officers' quarters. Not bad at all. Looks like it might be a comfortable trip to who-knows-where. Huddled in one room, nobody was saying much, just trying to warm up, too scared to sack out alone in our own bunks.

Dinner time. We're to be guests at the captain's table. Pack of hungry refugees pile on in and plop down. Kim sat at the far end of the table, away from the rest of us. He was already the loner in the group.

"Good evening, sir."

We greeted the captain, who didn't say anything. Just nodded and sat down. An interpreter joined us and we started some small talk with the captain about Russian food. He made a little hand motion towards two big flunkies who rushed over and laid it all out. Piles of salmon. Dig in!

Then came the vodka. Joe's eyes lit up. But what about my Coke?

"Say, unh, I don't drink hard stuff."

"But you *must* toast! The captain will be very disappointed if you do not toast to the success of your escape," says the interpreter.

Must toast, eh? Now we don't want to disappoint the captain, do we? In that case, I can probably force down a gulp or two.

We all toast our good luck. The captain toasts us. We toast him. Everybody toasts the interpreter, who toasts us back. Please, no more! I'm about ready to fall on my ass with all this toasting.

Captain claps his hands and a flunky brings another bottle of Russian firewater.

"The captain saves this only for special occasions. Because he is happy for you and honored to have you as guests, he challenges you to drink this strong liquor with him. It's almost straight alcohol."

Pure poison? No thanks, Ivan. I have to beg out of this one. Joe had been the busiest guy in our group with all this vodka toasting. But even he had the sense to back out.

"Tell him I'll take his challenge."

Wise-ass kid Phil. Ready to try anything, no matter how stupid it is.

The captain poured a glassful for himself. Shoved some bread in his mouth, took a deep breath and gulped the shit down.

"Wwwrrrrgh!"

Bugged-eyed, we just sat and stared. After that growl, all eyes turned to Phil.

"I'll do it, man. No sweat."

Dumb punk.

The interpreter showed him what to do. Phil put a wad of bread in his mouth. A glass about half full of the poison was placed in front of him. *Shooonk.* It was down.

"How do you feel?"

"All right, man."

The captain was a real military type, who wanted to get straight back to his work. No more partying. He said good night. We thanked him and he split for the bridge.

Phil still hadn't made it out of his chair. As the ship rocked in one direction, he swayed in the other. His face was turning bright red.

"Better get our big-ass hero back to the room."

He stood up and hit the floor in the same movement.

"Carry the dumb fuck back."

There isn't a hell of a lot to do as honored guests on a Soviet Coast Guard ship. We spent most of our time playing cards. Phil and I took turns as the blackjack bank. Kim stayed by himself. Either he was asleep in his bunk or sitting alone in a corner of the dining room. Sometimes he didn't even bother to come out for meals.

The trip lasted four days and nights. I could never keep track of what time it was. In the middle of one night, I became very thirsty and went out on a hunt for some fruit juice. Crept down the hall and into the unlit dining room. Maybe one of the guys in the kitchen could give me something to drink.

"Mr. Whitmore?"

Who the fuck is that?

"Over here in the corner, Mr. Whitmore."

It was our interpreter, sitting alone in the dark. A stud with his robe and cigarette holder.

"Do you want something?"

"I was looking for something to drink."

"That can be arranged. Do you have some time for a little chat?"

He spoke very softly and slowly.

"Yeah, I guess so."

What does this big Russian motherfucker want to bullshit about at this time of the night? He poured some juice for me and we started to rap. He just asked questions and I answered them. Straight. Not about to jive with the man when he has me on one of his ships in the middle of one of his seas. We talked about Memphis, my family, ghetto life, sports. Didn't say much about the Nam.

"Guess it's time for me to go to bed. Thank you for your company, Mr. Whitmore."

And he slinked off.

"Where the hell have you been so long?"

"I, unh, met the interpreter and we had a little chat."

"You too?"

It seems that the interpreter had already had a little chat with every other guy. But I was the only one with enough nerve to admit it.

"I guess he's all right. You think he's all right?"

We all looked around at each other and didn't say much more about it. The guys went back to playing cards.

Nothing happened during those four days. All we saw through our porthole windows were icebergs floating by. Not too encouraging. Then we spotted land.

"Gentlemen, pack your bags. You will go ashore in a few minutes."

A tugboat came to pick us up. It was only dawn. Wet and cold. Standing on the dock was the biggest man I've ever seen.

He was the driver of one of the three cars waiting to take us across this island to an airport. But first a stop at a hospital for Pappy's leg. A woman doctor examined him.

"You'll live."

She was cool. Spotted Pappy for a jerk.

After breakfast, we drove to the airport to catch a plane for about an hour's ride to the mainland. Not a word about where we're headed, how long we'd be there or where we'd finally be living.

The shock was waiting for us at the next airport. Mobs of people, photographers, little girls with flowers. This made for quite a change from being fugitives. We didn't know how to react. "Thank you, thank you" was about all we could say.

And there we met Mike. A short, chubby Russian with a great sense of humor. He was our interpreter-guide throughout all the Soviet Union.

I never did find out what the hell the name of that city was. They whipped us off on a tour of it with Mike translating. He was about as bored as we were. After lunch and some more goddamn toasting, we boarded another plane. This one was a huge mother, packed with families and their pots and pans, kids, chickens in crates. What a nuthouse! Mark said it was like a third-class Spanish railroad car. I had never seen one of those, but I guess they're a mess too. The people in the Soviet Union do a lot of their traveling this way because their country is so damn big.

"Where we going?"

"Moscow."

Moscow! That's supposed to be the center of the whole Communist world. Holy shit! We were scared, no matter how nice they'd been to us.

On the plane, we had our own little room. Just like a European railway. After a five-minute roll, the big motherfucker finally got off the ground.

Then Kim started to wise-mouth after six days of silence.

"You know that you're just a bunch of chickenshit punks."

What's this?

"You candy asses are only cowards, that's all."

"Now just what the fuck are you talking about?"

"You have no reason to desert. I'm the only one who has a good reason. Why did you leave? Go ahead, tell me why?"

Tell you why? Who the hell are you to be asking why? There is no good reason on earth why we have to give anyone a reason for what we do with our own lives. Who's side are you on anyway, Kim?

"Kim, we're all vets from Nam. Terry's been shot up and won some medals. What the hell are you breaking balls about?"

Joe was pissed at Kim. None of us could really figure Kim out other than he was just an oddball. Phil tried hard to make friends with Kim during the rest of the trip. Always giving him a special invitation to join us whenever we did anything.

After arriving in Moscow, we checked into a large downtown hotel. The joint was crawling with diplomats from all over the world. And Americans. We decided to fit right in and play the role of big-time tourists. This is when we met the boys.

The boys were plainclothes cops assigned to keep us out of trouble, carry our luggage, see to it that we ate on time and got to where we were supposed to be going. They were right out of a gangster movie. Three of them. All packing .38s under their jackets. Never taking off their hats, with the front brim always creased down.

"American cineema . . . I love you."

That was all one dude could say in English. And he said it whenever he had the chance. American cineema . . . I love you! I love you! Not hello, good-bye, good morning, thank you. Just, American cineema . . . I love you.

Christ, this is going to be a real cartoon. We called him Al Capone because those Russian names were too difficult to pronounce. The other cop looked like Tennessee Ernie Ford. A third dude, Snake, was the slippery kind who frequently disappeared.

Lunch. More toasts. A quick drive-around-look-see tour of Moscow.

Before dinner, we piled into the hotel bar for a few beers by ourselves and our first contact with the black market. On every street in the USSR, the market is always just around the corner.

"Dollar? You sell dollar?"

He couldn't say much more in English than "dollar." Phil decided to play games with him.

"Yeah, we got millions. What do we swap for? Lenin's tomb? Hey, you guys meet my buddy."

As we bought him beers, he was grinning ear to ear. Get rich on these Yankee assholes! We just signed for everything, so he figured that we were definitely the last of the big-time spenders.

Time for dinner.

"Phil, get rid of that clown."

He wanted to tag along with us. Now if Al Capone catches us messing with this black-market dude, we're in for an ass-chewing.

Capone was standing right outside the bar and spotted the hustler immediately.

"My friend. My friend."

Phil is trying to tell Capone that this hustler is his buddy. Capone let his jacket fly open and put his hands on his hips. Then the hustler saw that he was packing a .38.

Shooom. Through the lobby and out the front door. That hustler was gone. Capone shook his head as if trying to tell us what naughty boys we had been.

At dinner we found out that our little gang of bodyguards were from all over the Soviet Union. Capone was from Moscow. Tennessee Ernie lived in Georgia. Snake was from somewhere near Mongolia. And Mike came from Ukrania in the west. We sat around swapping stories about our home towns. They promised us that we could visit all their home republics. It was no joke. We did.

For almost four weeks, we flew around the Soviet Union as

the guests of a Soviet peace group. They wanted us to see as much of their country as possible. This was all very kind of them, but we still didn't know where the hell we would be spending the rest of our lives. This worrying took most of the fun out of touring. If I'd have known that it would be only a four-week tour before settling in Sweden, it would have been a hell of a lot more enjoyable.

My mind wasn't on Lenin's tomb, or the October Revolution or some Siberian deer who ran over a mountain and had a city named after him. Where the hell am I going to live . . . what about tomorrow when all this sight-seeing shit ends . . . and the day after tomorrow, when my real life begins? If I'm going to be an immigrant, it would be nice to know ahead of time in what country, before being dropped on it. Russia and its history and its mountains and its museums and its booze and even, but not quite, its broads didn't interest me one goddamn bit. I'm not a fat-cat American tourist; I'm a refugee from America and an immigrant to somewhere. So the sooner these Russians let me get down to some real living in my new country—wherever it is —the happier I'll be.

The Russians certainly had some good propaganda reasons for dragging us all over their country, from one town hall to the next. But we were getting a big favor in return—a one-way ticket and a safe-conduct pass to our new home. We weren't too hip on bullshitting about politics, so all they could do was to stick us behind a dinner table, introduce us as six young Americans who refused to return to Nam, blahsie, blahsie, blahsie, sit down, eat and get drunk. We were probably better excuses for partying than for making propaganda. But they sure managed to squeeze a shitload of tourist mileage out of us. If they weren't too busy getting smashed on their asses with vodka or wine, they'd be flying or driving us from one boring tourist spot to the next.

Our Russian guides and guards had a competition among themselves. Whose republic was best. Who made the best wine. Where were the prettiest broads. Who drinks the most vodka. And which city had the best circus.

During one of our first afternoons in Moscow, we were guests in a ringside box at the circus. Circuses are circuses. No big deal. Every clown in the place had to do something funny in front of us. Ha-ha, but where the hell are the chicks? We were a bunch of very horny bastards after all that traveling. Enough of this circus and sight-seeing shit, bring on the broads!

"You like this Moscow circus?"

"Yeah, it's nice."

"Well, I think that our circus is better. Leningrad circus is much better."

Jabber jabber jabber in Russian, and two of them start a friendly argument about circuses.

"You should see. Look well at this circus. Then you shall see. Compare."

The dude from Leningrad splits. Back in fifteen minutes.

"Gentlemen, we shall go now."

"Go where?"

"We shall see another circus."

"This one is O.K." We weren't up for leaving on another trip.

But off we go. Down to the waiting cars and drive off. To the airport! What the hell kind of circus do they have at the airport?

"Gentlemen, in about one hour we shall be in Leningrad."

And the whole goddamn gang piled aboard one of their railroad-car planes for Leningrad. To see another circus! I shit you not, we sat through another circus in Leningrad that evening.

Six assholes popping in and out of limousines, planes, box seats. Surrounded by flunkies. We caught more eyes wherever we went—like we were Kosygin's cousins.

"Gentlemen, your cars are waiting."

Right on, babe, right on! God only knows what we're doing or where we're going next.

In Leningrad, they put us up at a very modern hotel specially reserved for diplomats. And only a few blocks from a girls' school dormitory! Big mothers and none of them could speak a word of English. Times were hard.

Pappy had a clipping from *Pravda* about us which really blew their minds. I guess it was Pappy's only ticket to a piece of ass. The guys spent most of their free time in Leningrad at this dorm. Whenever we could, Joe and I split from the group to go on the prowl. There wasn't much free time.

"Today, you gentlemen may speak to the international press."

O.K. Why not? Fortunately or unfortunately, it wasn't a completely international press. The journalists were from Eastern Europe. They did a lot of poking.

"Isn't it true that there are only black men on the front lines in Vietnam?"

"No. Most black soldiers are in combat, but blacks and whites are together on the front."

This kind of questioning pissed me off. I felt that I had lots of good reasons for leaving and starting a new life elsewhere. But it was my own business and I didn't have to come out with any bullshit reasons which weren't true. Most of the guys felt this way, except Pappy and Kim. They did almost all the talking at the press conference and on the TV panel show that night.

Pappy had been nothing but a goddamn E-4 cook on an Army barge in Nam. But he was telling more lies about combat than I could even imagine. One story had a woman camera operator crying so hard, she had to leave the studio. This was too much for us. Right on the air, we told him to keep it straight or shut up.

His worst story was about an officer who had ordered an enlisted man to shoot a baby. When the grunt refused, the officer shot them both. We all knew goddamn well that no officer would dare to shoot an enlisted man on an operation with enlisted guys around. The other dudes would kill the officer immediately, even if they had hated the grunt who was murdered by the officer. Pappy was just spilling out a lot of shit because he needed the attention.

Toward the end of the show, Kim started to rap about dropping nuclear bombs on America. That would solve all the world's problems. One of the translators blew up at this.

"Son, are you crazy? No country must ever use nuclear

weapons! The Soviet Union and the United States must never use these bombs. They would only destroy the entire world and solve nothing."

That shut up Kim and surprised all of us. Kim had some kind of a strange bug up his ass, but we never figured out what it was.

No more press conferences after that. Just tours, toasts, trains and planes. We seemed to be coming in or out of Leningrad or Moscow every other day. It was getting to be a hell of a drag. Especially for Joe and me. Never alone. Too many politicians. And no girls.

On the day before Lenin's birthday, Leningrad was packed with tourists for the big parade. In the hotel bar, I ran into my first black cat.

"Hey brother, where you from?"

"Ethiopia."

"Oh yeah. Say, you wouldn't happen to know where all the women are hiding around this town?"

"They're everywhere. You just have to look a little."

So long as I know they're available. Thank you, brother, I'm on my way.

Joe and I knew that we were almost always watched by one of Capone's boys. If we're going out, we have to sneak out.

There's a crowd in the lobby. They're heading for the front door. Drift into the middle of the crowd and we're on our way out with them. Right into a waiting cab and we're off. Watch out, Ivan, gonna get your sister's ass!

"Girls, man, girls."

The cabbie didn't understand a word of English. Joe drew some tits and asses in the air and he got the message.

We stopped in front of another hotel. From the supply of rubles given to us for pocket money, Joe layed a few on the cabbie for his services.

No sooner were we out of that cab, than two women swept us up and down the street. As unbelievable as it sounds, two big but young broads grabbed us immediately. Not that we were any great sex stars; it was just to get away from two drunks who had followed them out of the hotel. After playing these two dudes out of all their coins, the broads were looking for some fast excuses to get away. Us.

"What the hell we got ourselves into now?"

"You Americans?"

"Yeah, baby."

The magic word—Americans! Into a cab and the four of us are cuddling up.

"Where can we get some booze? Vodka?"

Joe is itching to party. The chick who spoke English gave the driver a few rubles and some instructions. He grumbled a little but stopped to buy the booze. After wandering down an alley, he fell back out with a bottle of bootleg vodka.

"Where do we go?"

"I don't know, baby, how about your place?"

"No, no. We must go to her house."

Figuring that we're a couple of dumb, rich American tourists, the driver wanted to double up on the price. No, Jack, that American we are not. My broad swore a blue streak of Russian curses. He settled for the right price.

Her place was out in the suburbs in a large block of modern apartment houses. A ground-floor flat and the front door is locked. So she beats on the window.

"Goddamn, tell her to stop the racket before the neighbors start throwing shit out the windows."

She was trying to wake up whoever was in there.

Crack—tinkle . . . she broke the window. That does it. Now these drunken broads will have all our asses in jail for breaking and entering.

"What the fuck did you get me out of bed for?"

Or something like that in Russian. Some big dude had opened the door after the window fell in.

"Who's he?"

"Her brother."

Well, if he doesn't mind, we don't mind. No time to be bashful. Joe broke out the vodka and they all went to it. Goddamn, but those Russian broads could really do their thing on that booze. I still have one eye on them and one on brother Ivan, who is a very big guy. The dude wasn't saying much, too busy drinking. He got the word in Russian to shut up, put your clothes on and get out. These Russian women don't mess around with being polite.

O.K., babe, now show me how you do it Soviet style. Into the bedroom for a little business discussion.

"No, baby, I ain't got that much."

Money, that is. They were professional hustlers and hoped to take two sucker Americans for all they could get. We bargained and slid around and finally reached an agreement. Joe was making his bid in the living room. There was only one bed in the place.

Luckily for me, it was cheap. Because Russian babes just can't make it in the sack for love or money. Even an icy Swede is better than one of those big Russian mamas.

"Take your time. Take your time. We play."

Play? I just want to get my nut off and split.

Oh no, not that fast, not yet . . . she's blowing me! Goddamn, I'm too horny for that stuff right now. Whew . . . she stopped just in time. Nice, but why waste it.

She was a big woman. I didn't realize how big until she put her knees up around her head. Yeah, those Russian babes are *big* women!

We fell into our thing and finished while Joe was still bargaining in the living room.

"Hey, Whit, we got a visitor."

Brother Ivan had returned!

Oh, I do hope brother is broad-minded, because from where he's standing he has a wide-screen view of me and this babe lying bare ass to ass in the sack and Joe and his sister on the living-room floor.

"Her brother knows the facts of life, don't he?"

Not a word from anyone. He strolls into the bedroom and starts to poke around in the closet. The babe sits up. Then it all broke loose.

First they start screaming at each other. Where's my fucking pants? Joe, stop laughing, you ballbreaker.

Kaboom! A chair into the wall. Goddamn, where are my shoes? That motherfucker is bound to grab one of us soon. Had it up, Whit, had it up now!

The bitch ran for the telephone. Never made it. He kicked her dead in the ass and sent her sprawling across the living-room floor. Snatched the phone right out of the wall.

"Joe, move your ass before he kills us!"

"No man, cool it. This shit is funny."

Funny? Some fucked-up sense of humor. Brother is tearing pictures off the walls, the dining-room table is flipped. No, Joe, he ain't funny.

Then brother stops to catch his breath. What's this madman going to do next?

He starts to put everything back in place! Cool as a clam, he turned the table right side up, replaced the cloth, put the pictures on the wall. What kind of nut is this?

"Look at this funny motherfucker, Whit."

I'm looking. He's brushing his hand over my head—you're damn right I'm looking. If he makes a quick move, it's kick and run. He's too big to fight.

"Whit, this big ape better leave soon, 'cause I ain't had my piece of ass yet."

"Ask him to go buy more booze."

The girls liked that idea. Joe layed five rubles on the dude. Vodka? Now we're speaking his language. He took the bread and split.

No sooner was he out the door than Joe was in the sack legging his broad. He wasn't kidding when he said he was horny.

After all the sports were over, we asked the girls about the madman.

"Would somebody tell us what that was all about?"

"He is her brother and my husband."

Ulp . . . her old man! My bitch's old man caught me with his wife. Now I know that these Russians don't think like Swedes. Salt mines for me, baby. That son of a bitch is coming back with a cop and I'm getting ten years for dicking his wife!

"He knows what we do, but sometimes he gets angry. You drink with him and everything O.K."

I'm not that thirsty.

"Joe, let's had it up while we still got the chance."

"Stick around. I think we can get another piece of ass on the house."

"We did enough screwing for one day and we got a plane to catch."

We didn't have much time left to make it back to the hotel and meet the gang. They were flying us down to Georgia that afternoon. If we're going to be on time, we have to go by cab. Not a cab in sight. Hoof it. All the way back to the hotel. No food, no sleep. We were beat to the ass.

"Where is everybody?"

Gone. All of them had left. The parade for Lenin was over and they were on their way to Georgia. A cleaning lady showed us to a room where our baggage was stored. Now what? Sleep. Then we'll come up with an idea.

While I slept, Tennessee Ernie came in.

"Where you go? How you go? You CIA. You CIA!"

Joe caught all the shit. Mike arrived just in time to rescue us.

"That was very foolish. What did you do?"

We gave him a quick rundown and he laughed.

"I would have done the same thing."

All the Russian boys liked Leningrad because it was a big action town with lots of loose broads. Good-looking by Russian standards.

Before leaving for Georgia, Mike gave us some papers to fill out. They were like military "dream sheets." Where do we want to go and live. Joe and I said Finland. The others wanted Canada, except Kim, who chose Czechoslovakia. The Russians said nothing about where we would actually go. I'm sure they knew it would have to be Sweden, but they wanted us to feel like we could have some choice.

Why Finland? Well, we'd heard that it was a neutral country. Although it had fought on the side of the Nazis against the Soviet Union, Finland wasn't fighting any more wars now. We were sick and tired of traveling, so Finland looked even better because it was sitting right next to Russia, just a hop, skip and jump from Leningrad. I'd never heard about any racial problems in Finland—maybe they'd even like me, get a big kick out of me being the only black Finn. What the hell, *one* black man is no threat. What we didn't know then was that Finland is a poor country—no work. A hell of a lot of Finns have to come to Sweden for work, where—believe it or not—they are Sweden's "niggers," get the shit jobs, live in small ghettos. Some Swedes call them *"finndjävlar,"* which means something like "fucking Finns" or "Finnish bastards." But at least the Finns aren't dragged into Sweden in chains and they are paid for their work—which puts them a few steps higher than my ancestors in America. And there are no Swedes bombing Finnish churches and shooting Finns or lynching them—so they're even better off than my brothers and sisters in America today.

But Finland was just dreaming for Joe and me. We didn't know anything about the scene in Scandinavia then, that Sweden is really the only Scandinavian country that can afford to take in refugees. It works out to be a good deal for the Swedes, because they get all the workers they need and a chance to look "humanitarian" at the same time.

Down in Georgia it was all wine drinking and tours. The gang was ahead of us somewhere. Just Mike, Joe and I on the wino special. Dinners, wine, speeches, wine, tours, wine. The shit was coming out of my ears by the time we left Georgia for the Black Sea.

"We thought we lost you clowns in Siberia."

Thanks for the welcome. Back with the boys. The Black Sea

was more of the same tour crap with lots of sun added. Those goddamn tours were driving me crazy. I didn't know what the hell they were talking about and cared less. But the worst was back in Leningrad.

"Who's Lenin?"

Asshole. I had never even heard of the guy. But after those tours, we had seen everything about him and what he did, including his shitter.

The only time one of those tour guides ever got to me with a spiel was at a mass grave near Leningrad where the Nazis had passed through and killed everybody. She almost had me in tears. The Russian people had really suffered in the second world war. Although I had never heard anything about it until I went there.

After all that touring around, it came as a big relief when they sent us to a sports camp up north.

"We're going to get you away from girls and liquor for a while. Improve your health."

Mike was jiving with us. Get away from broads? Sure, we played a lot of soccer and volleyball and always lost to the Russians, but I still managed to pop a chick on a picnic table in the woods. And Joe got his vodka from somewhere.

It was up there in the fresh-air-country scene where they laid the big news on us.

"You will be allowed to live in Sweden. In a few days, a plane will take you to Stockholm."

HEJ, SVERIGE!

Sweden. Where's that? I don't know. The cat says Sweden, so we go to Sweden. Where else? Certainly not Russia, the world's dullest country, all booze and boredom. James Bond must have been bullshitting us about that place. And Sweden sure as hell must be better than the States or Nam as far as I'm concerned, so why *not* Sweden? Well, for one thing, it's a country of blond-haired, blue-eyed *white* people. So I wasn't completely without my doubts about Sweden.

At the airlines terminal in Leningrad, things became a little jumpy. The Soviet peace group had given us three hundred dollars apiece to take care of our needs for the first few weeks in Stockholm. We stocked up on tax-free goodies while they were still available. In Stockholm we would be met by the Swedish-Vietnam Committee and the American Deserters Committee, who were supposed to help us get our feet on the ground. But before reaching Stockholm, we ran into our first Swede right in the Leningrad terminal. One of those big Viking motherfuckers, our SAS copilot or steward. He hit us with a strongman inter-rogation routine.

"How much money do you each have?"

"Three hundred American dollars."

"I want to see it."

See it? What the hell for . . . O.K., we'll be cool. It's your country, so if you want to fuck with us some, we're not about to give you any jive back-talk.

"You all must realize that you suffer the consequences if my country decides not to accept you. Then you must pay your way back to the country you came from."

Back to Russia? Never. O.K., Svensson, I'll be nice. But please let me in.

A big Russian was standing in the background, listening to all this shit.

"Don't worry. He has no authority and knows nothing. By Swedish law, they *must* take you."

By Swedish law, eh . . . and a Russian is saying that the Swedes *must* take us and Russia is a hell of a lot bigger than Sweden, so I think we'll take the Russian's word for it.

Sweden officially began to admit American Vietnam war refugees in January, 1968. Although several draft resisters and deserters were already living in Sweden before that time, nothing was public until the Intrepid Four showed up around Christmas, 1967. The publicity those cats received helped guys who were fed up with all the shit in Nam and refused to do any more killing for Sam. Now they knew there was at least one country in the world which would let them live like human beings— Sweden. The Swedes call it "humanitarian asylum." This means that they will allow a person to live at peace in Sweden if his own country is forcing him to kill other human beings in war which he sincerely believes is immoral, unjust, illegal—in other words, if there is no goddamn good reason for all the killing he refuses to do.

Well, I sure as hell had been involved in enough killing in the Nam to have that belief. Nobody can ever tell me that the war in Vietnam is not immoral. It was disgusting and I'm none too proud that I was once a part of killing women and their children when my country was supposed to be there to help them. No more of that shit for me, Jack. Thank God that the Swedes have this law. I don't know much about laws, but it doesn't take a goddamn lawyer to know that what's happening in Nam is dead wrong and that the Swedish law is just plain common sense. That's one thing the Swedes usually have a lot of—common sense. So hang on, all you Vikings, you got some soul coming your way.

Limousining it out to the airport. Riding in high style. Enjoy it while you can, boys, it ain't lasting forever. Then the bear hugs and kisses. Our Russian guards and guides said good-bye to us in the typical Russian way—bear hugs and kisses. That cheek kissing was bad enough, but when it came to those bear hugs, I was hoping the dudes wouldn't get carried away. Mike even had tears in his eyes. He had been with us for the entire journey, especially with Joe and me.

"You tough U. S. Marines? We see how tough."

That was how he used to jive with us; Mike always wanted to arm wrestle. And he always won. He had the biggest, most "bodacious" hands I'd ever seen. Real bone-crackers. With all that jiving around, the three of us had become close raps. It wasn't easy to say good-bye to that big bear with tears in his eyes.

After all the kissing and hugging, we were the last ones on the plane again. Six on the aisle, one in back of the other. And there they were—Swedish stewardesses. According to legend, the world's sexiest broads! My first look at the real thing. Hummmm. Long legs in short blue skirts. Not bad. In Russia the view was all short legs in long skirts. Each time one of those blue skirts passed by, five heads automatically appeared in the aisle to eyeball the long legs. Kim was the only one not interested in the scenery.

"Now that's good coffee!"

An American. Sitting right next to me and drinking his coffee. Why do I have all the luck?

"Yeah, it's better than the Russian stuff."

Play along with him and maybe he won't bother me while I try to catch a few z's. My eyes were shut, but I couldn't sleep. All kinds of ideas were running through my head. This is it, my final destination. Home. Not Memphis but Stockholm. Not the family I had lived with for eighteen years, not the baby girl I had fathered, but a new family. Not the block and the brothers and sisters, but Sweden—please, God, may they not hate me here too. This must be the only place on earth where it even *looks* like I have a chance to make it on my own.

The Russian peace group told us that Sweden hadn't been at

war in over 150 years—and that time it was against the Czar. So at least they're not going to be shoving a gun in my hand and sending me off to be a grunt again. That much I could be sure of, but what about . . . the lucky lady. Who will she be? That's right, I was thinking about a wife. Why not? If this is going to be my home, I want a family. It will have to be a Swedish broad. So she'll probably be blonde, blue-eyed, with a funny Viking name like Erika or Britt, barely able to speak English, big tits, long legs. Little did I know then that she'd have dark hair, rap jive soul-talk as fast as I could, have a name like Chiquita and a young, lovely brown-skinned daughter, who would call me "Papa" and speak not a word of English. No, that's not what I was expecting on that plane ride to Stockholm.

"Hey, Whit, I hear Swedes ain't too fond of brothers."

Joe woke me out of my dreaming.

"What do you mean they ain't too fond?"

"Yeah, it's true. There ain't no black people in Sweden. They're as bad as them Mississippi motherfuckers."

Shit. Ain't there nowhere I can go and be at peace? What the hell am I going to do if I can't be allowed to live an ordinary life just like everybody else in Sweden? It's bad enough to be a foreigner in any country, but if they hold my color against me even after I've been living there fifty years—then what? I can never go back to America; I don't want to ever go back to America. At least five years at hard labor in a Marine prison and then the rest of my life as a black ex-con—not because I killed someone but because I refused to kill any more? No thanks. I just have to take Sweden as it comes. If I don't want to fight in Sam's wars, then I have to live in whichever country will have me and make the best of it. At least I won't be starting out as a slave for some Swede. But I still have to live with Swedes. . . . Joe, I hope to God that you're wrong. I had pictured the Swede as a big sailor in a black turtleneck sweater and skipper's hat. A mean hardass, no jiving cat. Now if he doesn't groove on me and if I have to live the rest of my life in his country without a woman, without a family . . . well shit—it ain't too cool. I was one scared brother.

Arlanda. Stockholm's international airport. The same scene all over again. Photographers, flashbulbs popping, newsmen, a million questions. No translators needed this time, it was all in English. Have you really been to Vietnam? What did you do there? Why did you leave? Are you a Communist? Are you a Communist?

"Why the hell are you asking that?"

"Well, you've been to the Soviet Union."

These motherfuckers are dumber than I am. If they're supposed to know what a Communist is, how can they ask me such a stupid question just because I've traveled through the Soviet Union?

"I'm not talking. I'm not saying a goddamn word as long as AP and UPI are in this room."

Joe was breaking balls.

"Hey, Joe, who's AP and UPI?"

"They're goddamn American newsmen and you know they won't write anything but bullshit about us."

Everybody shut up. The press conference was over unless the Americans left the room. The Swedish-Vietnam Committee got a kick out of this.

"We'll talk with anybody but Americans."

Joe wasn't jiving and he wasn't wrong. It all came out later that most of the American correspondents in Stockholm used to work for the CIA. One was the press officer at the American Embassy, one is still the Scandinavian reporter for Voice of America and another guy is a Radio Free Europe man! All this while working at the same time for civilian newspapers, radio and TV stations. Now you just know that they're not about to bite the hand that feeds them. There must be a lot of bullshit written in the States about Sweden—and about us—if they get all their information from these assholes.

So we only talked to the Swedish newspapers. As it turned out, they gave us a fair shake.

Now it's time to meet the man. Passport police. One at a time we were led into their office. More questions.

"Terry Whitmore?"

"That's me."

"Are you a Communist?"

"No, I'm no Communist."

Goddamnit, why are they always asking me about communism? I can tell them all they want to know about Lenin and his shitter, but don't ask me about communism, because I'm not even sure what the hell it is! Russia is a dull place where they do a lot of drinking—that's all I know.

Where were you born? Where were your parents born? Your mother's maiden name? Your father's occupation? Your grandparents' names? Your grandmothers' maiden names? Now hold on a minute, how am I supposed to know all this shit. My grandmothers were probably slaves when they were kids. I don't know their goddamn maiden names.

"Uuh, Rosie. Rosie Lee."

I've got to be nice to this motherfucker. He's the man and it's his country. Got me right by the balls. I'll tell him all the goddamn names he wants to hear. I don't know my grandma's name, but if he wants one, he'll get one.

"Yeah and the other one's name was Susie. Susie Johnson."

Asshole.

Then he wanted to know how much schooling I had and if my parents were rich. Guess he didn't know too much about black people in Memphis.

"What did you do in Vietnam?"

"I was an infantryman in the Marines."

"No technical training?"

"Nope. Just how to shoot a rifle and an M.79 grenade launcher."

"Why do you not want to go back to Vietnam and America?"

Now that's a hell of a question. You got a few hours to spare?

I told him briefly that I felt the war in Nam was wrong and that I didn't want to be killing any more Vietnamese or be killed by them. There was no reason for me to be in Vietnam. And if I went back to America now, they'd throw me in prison. Then I started to tell him about a black man's life in America.

"That is not why the Swedish government allows Americans to live here. It is only because of the Vietnam war."

I suppose if the Swedes let black Americans in because America is hell for black men, there would be a million blacks sailing over here tomorrow. Eldridge Cleaver can't even come here for a visit, so they're not about to have open house for brothers.

"In about ten weeks, you will receive a decision from the Aliens' Commission. They will give you labor and residence permits then. Before that time, you are not allowed to work."

Thank God for that three hundred dollars the Russians gave us.

"This way out, gentlemen."

Goddamn, more blue uniforms. This time it's the POLIS. Cops in Swedish.

The Russians had warned us that we might have to spend the first night or two in the can, because none of us had passports. They needed some time to shuffle around their papers with our grandmothers' names before declaring us safe and harmless enough to live in Sweden.

Very polite dudes. The Swedish cops carried our bags to their cars.

"You see that?"

"What?"

"The cop car."

A Plymouth. A goddamn American car. They don't even buy their own Volvos. Sam is everywhere. Even on the road to the police station in Märsta, it was Esso, Texaco, Gulf. That mother-fucking Sam had us surrounded.

The police must have had some doubts about Kim, because

they held him in the jail at Märsta and sent the rest of us else-where.

"Empty your pockets."

The man was playing this like the real thing, except for the hot meal ordered for us from a restaurant.

"They really locking us up? We really going to jail?"

Mark is crying again.

"Yeah, pussy, you better get up against the wall."

Joe spread-eagled himself against the wall so the cops could frisk him.

"Take it, babe. Take it all."

Everybody realized that Joe was only jiving except Mark, who started to do the same thing.

"I've never been in a jail before. Do you think they'll hold us long?"

"Shut up, shithead, and empty your pockets."

Before throwing us in our cells for the night, the cops let us watch Swedish TV. Then some of my fears about Sweden dis-appeared. There was Lou Rawls in Sweden and those white folks were really digging that black cat. Chicks all over him. No problem, babe; at least Sweden ain't Mississippi.

"Sorry, but you two have to sleep in here."

There weren't enough individual cells to go around, so Joe and I were stuck with the tank. The tank is where drunks and junkies are dumped.

"Yeah, we're sorry too."

They brought us some mattresses, so we didn't have to sleep on the bare floor.

"You got any smokes?"

"Nope. They took everything when we emptied our pockets."

"Call the man."

The man says we can't smoke in the cells.

"Say, uuh, can I get a book from my bag."

The man let Joe out of the cell to get his book. He came back with smokes.

"You got any matches?"

"Nope. I guess we'll have to chew them."

Joe was an old vet when it came to jail cells, after spending so much time in the Marine brig.

"I'll get a light the same way we got a light in the brig."

He squatted over the electrical socket and popped it by poking away with a small piece of metal.

"Asshole, you're gonna blow yourself up."

When the socket was hot enough, Joe lit his cigarette. American know-how does it again.

At two o'clock in the morning, we woke up.

"That fucking sun sure comes up early here."

It took me about a month to get used to sleeping through these goddamn early Scandinavian sunrises.

By the time real morning came around, some Americans from Stockholm had arrived in an old, beat up Volkswagen bus. When they came busting through that door, my heart jumped.

"Blood. Goddamn, we got some blood around here!"

A brother. A big, fat, beautiful black face hit that door and set my mind at ease.

"Brother, you ain't got no sweat from here on in. You're home free now. Nuthin' to worry about."

Right on, brother! I'm with you all the way. Now I can stop thinking so much about having gone too far, about having left behind the people I love, the people I'll probably never see again. Stop worrying about tomorrow and the day after tomorrow. I have some brothers in Sweden!

"We have to be helping each other and all the other brothers who are coming. Don't you worry about Sam no more. That's his war in Nam. Let him fight it."

I'm with you, babe, I'm with you all the way.

This time we're not coming in chains on a slave ship. We're immigrants! If there are brothers living in Sweden, we can help each other along, the way every other group of people who immigrated into America were able to help each other.

I just know I can make it now, babe! Start my life again. No more killing, no more ducking bullets, no more "You can't do that, nigger." Just a nice, quiet, ordinary life. Thank you, God, for getting me to Sweden and putting some brothers here with me!

MAKING IT

Stockholm. It could have been Dingdangadoo, Idaho, for all I knew about where the hell I was. The ADC old-timers drove us to their run-down dump of an office in the center of town.

"Where do you guys plan on staying tonight?"

"Where do *we* plan? I thought you dudes are supposed to be doing all the planning and arranging."

Some of the welcoming committee had their heads about ten feet up their political assholes. It looked as though we'd have to shift for ourselves in the beginning. And we did, for the most part.

I didn't have to hang around that hole in the wall very long, before Jay Wright came bopping on in.

"Hey, brother, what's happening?"

"Everything, man. They taking care of you here?"

"Shit, they can't even take care of themselves."

"You stick with me, brother."

Jay is one of the sharpest, shrewdest cats in Stockholm. A black from New Orleans, he had finished one tour in Nam for the U. S. Air Force and was headed back for another when he split.

"Where you going, Whit?"

"My brother here is looking after me. You white boys gonna have to take care of yourselves."

Beautiful. Brothers in Stockholm—out of sight. Everything is together now, babe.

Jay had a small pad just north of town in Solna. A cot was set up in the kitchen for me until I could find a place of my own. A tough job in Stockholm.

"You got some coins, Terry?"

"Yeah, a few."

"Then I'll show you the town tonight."

Check out the Swedish sights. First stop—Hamburger Bush. A club jumping with broads and a few brothers. This is my scene. Grooving, drinking my Coke, munching on my popcorn.

"Hej, Jay, *hur går det?"*

This chick asks Jay how's it going. Not bad. She and her friend pull up some chairs. Mmmmm . . . her friend is Swedish, but she sure doesn't look it. Black hair, brown eyes and she can rap English almost like any sister on the block. Chiquita. Stay cool . . . keep munching on my popcorn. Lots of chicks in this town. I can take my time.

But Chiquita wasn't going to give me a lot of time to play around. She didn't say much that night, but the big trap was being planned. And I was keeping so cool, I walked right into it with my eyes wide open.

Jay was supposed to split the next day on a trip to East Germany. Before he left, he put in a few calls to find a pad for me.

"You go see this woman tomorrow night. She wants to rent out a room or a small pad for the summer.

Groovy. Thank you, brother.

The joint cost me about a hundred kronor deposit and it was mine for three months. I'd have to wait just about that long before the Swedish Aliens' Commission would give me a labor permit. Until then, I wasn't allowed to work. Just study Swedish for a few hours a day and then . . . well, go on the prowl. Not a goddamn thing to do in Stockholm for a foreigner without a work permit—except put his pad to good use if he's lucky enough to have one.

It took five minutes to move everything I owned into the pad —one small bag. Headed back to Jay's about ten o'clock at night just as it started to get dark.

Bumph! She almost knocked me on my ass. Some wild-ass hippy chick was busting down the street screaming and screeching away.

"In that house . . . in that house . . . my girl friend!"

What house? What girl friend. What the hell is happening?

She's looking like an Apache Indian in her outfit and jumping up and down like she's on the warpath.

"Help me! Please help me!"

Some Swedish dude went flying by us. She tried to stop him for help, but he pretended we weren't even there.

O.K., baby, I'm a big, bad Marine. Always ready to help a lady in distress, especially if I think I can get a piece of ass out of the deal.

"Yeah, sure I'll help. What's the problem?"

"Somebody got my girl friend in that house."

Mmmm . . . that makes two pieces of ass. I didn't know anything about hippie broads, but they couldn't be too different from other women. And my first legging in Sweden was overdue.

The house looked like something out of a Frankenstein movie. Boarded-up windows, about eight different roofs, maybe a hundred years old, weeds growing out of everything, dark inside, almost no furniture—and no people. And no noise. And the lights don't work. And I'm getting a little nervous. What the fuck is her girl friend doing in this joint?

"You live here?"

"No."

"Your friend live here?"

"No."

That means we're burglars. Nice way to kick off life in a new country.

"Keep your head low."

I think I'm back in the Nam.

"Where the hell is your girl friend? She ain't down on the floor nowhere."

This crazy broad is crawling along the floor with a match. She obviously isn't looking for her girl friend. But her ass is looking better to me all the time . . . and those tits! They're just swinging free in the breeze under her T-shirt.

She crawls around for about fifteen minutes. Goddamn, if something doesn't happen soon, I'm dragging her out of here, up to Jay's pad and into the sack.

"What the hell you lookin' for now?"

"My bag . . . my little bags."

I wasn't hip to any little bags. This broad is nuts, but if she wants to crawl around on the floor looking for little bags, goddamn, I'll crawl around with her. Anything to get out of this creepy joint faster.

Clunk. Her Indian bag fell off her shoulder and all its shit spilled across the floor. Real shit—needles, tissues, spoon. Christ, a fucking dope freak! Well, if she wants to shoot herself to death with that crap in her arm, that's her business. As long as I get my first piece of real Swedish ass soon. Very soon, because after a half-hour of crawling around, the only thing I was getting was a filthy suit.

Wheehaw . . . wheehaw . . . wheehaw . . . wheehaw . . . Sweet pleadin' Jesus, what kind of a fucking noise is that? Searchlight in the windows. A Swedish cop car's siren, that's what kind of noise. How in the hell did I get myself into this shit? In Sweden for only one day, trying to get political asylum, a black man in an all white country—and I'm caught red-handed with one of their Swedish daughters, an addict no less, and she's probably got some shit on her and we're in a house where we're not supposed to be . . . Please, dear God, may the Swedes not have a Siberia—though maybe even that would be better than throwing me out of the country. Asshole, how did you fuck up this time?

It's every man for himself now. So long, babe. I'm getting out while the getting's good. Went straight to the door and opened it. Play it straight and honest.

"Your identification, please."

"Tell him what happened. You explain."

Let her do the talking. She mumbled something in Swedish and showed them her I.D.

"You too."

But my I.D. is back in the Nam jungle.

"Look, you have everything on me in your files."

Off to the station house. Oh God, they're going to beat on

me but good. But no, not a blow. The Swedish cops didn't lay a hand on me in the car or at the station. While I was expecting the old Memphis routine, these Swedish dudes weren't doing anything until they knew who I was and if I had done anything wrong.

"Roll up your sleeves."

They got her now. I'm standing right next to her at the desk, hanging my head. Well, at least they can never get me for that shit. Her arms were full of holes.

"How long have you been in Sweden?"

"One day."

That's all they asked me. A dude got on the phone and made about four or five calls. The broad and the cop were laughing with each other. What kind of a police station is this?

"You take your girl. You can go now."

Take my girl? Go? Say no more . . . *hej då!* I'm gone.

The chick was a registered addict so they let her go. My story checked out, so they let me go. Now to get down to some business.

"Say, baby, you can come back to my place now."

"I must go back and find my bag."

Crazy fucking freak! *Hej då,* good-bye. You go search for your little bag, but this time without me. No piece of ass is worth that much trouble.

My summer pad was about two yards long by two yards wide. The only time I could stay in it was to sleep. Otherwise, it drove me nuts.

"Man, you gotta come out and meet some groovy people."

Joe Kametz to the rescue. He had met several Swedish families who lived on Söder, the southern part of Stockholm. Two of them were very active Swedish pacifists who were interested in helping American refugees get settled. They were having a little party to which Joe and I were invited. That's nice, meet some Swedes, see their family life, relax.

They had a big, groovy pad—about six rooms, two baths.

Joe was boarding there—free, until he received his labor permit.

What a party! I wasn't in the place more than two minutes when some broad cornered me and started in with a thousand questions about American Indians. Hell, what do I know about Indians?

"It's hard enough to find out about my own people's history in America. Don't ask me about Indians, lady."

"Do you know what happened to the American Indian who shot some white people in Vietnam? They framed him for murder. Unjust. I know it was unjust and I wrote to the Pentagon about it."

These Swedes do a hell of a lot of letter writing to other countries. Sometimes I wish they'd do some writing to their own government to help the foreigners who are getting pushed around in Sweden. But I didn't know enough about the situation to say anything then. And I was still a guest in a Swede's house and in his country without a work permit.

The social chitchat doesn't last too long at a Swedish party. Swedes usually don't have too much to say. Until they break out the booze. Then back off, baby, all hell is about to bust loose! Nobody, but nobody in this world can down that juice like the Swedes. The Russians drink a lot over a long period of time and get shit-faced slowly. The Swede attacks that bottle like he's raping a broad! Bam—it's all gone and he's on his ass. Blabbering, slobbering away for the rest of the night.

The booze never interested me much. Broads. That's my idea of a good time. Single broads. Married ones have husbands, and husbands mean trouble where I come from.

At this particular party, all the broads, all three of them, had husbands, and their husbands all had bottles of vodka. Some party.

Typical scene. I'm the only black in the place, so the talk naturally turns to black people. It happens every time. A thousand white people and only one black cat in the place? Same old shit, they'll start talking about black people.

"You know that the most beautiful man I'd ever seen was a Negro in New York."

You don't say? This is a *dude* rapping to me with a few shots of brännvin, Swedish vodka, under his belt.

"If I had been a homosexual, I'd have given myself to him right on the spot."

Goddamn! What the hell kind of odd asses do I have to be living with for the rest of my life? Keep a stone face. Stay cool. Say nothing, just sip my orange soda while they guzzle that vodka.

Then it happens. Some chick walks over to a dude, not her husband, and runs her fingers up and down his pants. Nothing! I see nothing. Say nothing. Do nothing. This is their country and their way of doing things. If one of their traditions is standing on their heads and pissing on the wall, that's fine by me. Just don't ask me to join the fun.

No such luck. Like I said, I'm the only black at this small Swedish party, so I'm not about to blend into the woodwork. While Running Fingers is working over the other chick's husband, old Lisa Long Legs moves in on me. The only black man in the place. How lucky can I get? Back on the block, I'd get a razor in my back about this time. Check the exits because I may have to had it out fast.

"Black people have beautiful hair. I love your hair."

"Uuh, yeah."

Where's her husband? Sure, I have one eye on her, but the other eye is glued on goddamn Eric the Red over in the corner.

"I think white people have beautiful hair too."

What the hell else am I going to say? But please don't stand so damn close.

"How tall are you?"

"Over six feet."

Maybe I can get her into a mathematics conversation.

"Unh, what's six feet in centimeters?"

"Stand next to me and I'll compare."

Oh God, where is that exit? Body rubbing. If Eric catches this action, he'll be seeing red, not black. This is my first experience at home with Swedes. What the hell is going on? Another broad is standing behind me now; *she* wants to see how tall I am! One poor-ass black cat sandwiched between two big white blondes, and their white husbands are in the same room!! Ooooheee, please go away! But it's no big thing. These dudes are just staring at me like they don't give a shit. Make yourself at home!

"Um, um, I . . . unh . . . have to go out to buy some cigarettes. Bye."

I stayed out for about an hour to buy those cigarettes. One very scared cat. It's going to take a long time for me to get used to this place. They may let me live here and let me work and go about my own business and not force me into any wars, but these Swedes sure have some weird customs.

When I came back to the pad, everybody had sacked out except Running Fingers and Eric. They were going at it hot and heavy in the living room.

"Excuse me."

"That's O.K.," and she winks at me. While she's slapping one on Eric, she's winking at me.

Straight to bed. But I can't sleep a wink. These broads are walking back and forth all night long. If one of them had entered my room and tried some Swedish tricks on me, I don't know what the hell I'd have done. I was certainly too scared to get it up.

Those first few weeks in Sweden were just as weird as that night. Not that it's changed much since then. I've just learned to sit back, stay cool and laugh at whatever the hell these Swedes do when they're drunk. Because when they're sober, there's not much to laugh about.

So here I am in Sweden, Whit the Mover surrounded by broads who are hot to trot. Chicks are my favorite pastime, no matter what the time is. I should be diddling around enough to make Casanova look like a faggot. Well, I tried. And I wasn't doing too badly, until Chiquita put a stop to all that. Believe it or not, I am now a family man. In Sweden, of all places, where it's not exactly an easy job. So my life today is nothing to be writing books about.

Chiquita cornered me after a few weeks in Sweden. We started to meet often. Like every afternoon after work. Chiquita has a daughter by a black man. Fay. A lovely, brown, five-year-old girl who can't speak a word of English but calls me "Papa." Papa. That's what did it. I needed somebody here in Sweden. Somebody who knew the language, where to get honest jobs, how to get a place to live. Somebody who also spoke my language, liked my music, ate my kind of food and made me just plain happy to be where I was. And somebody to call me "Papa."

It was impossible at first. She was living at home with her parents. Apartments are hard as hell to get in Stockholm unless a lot of bread is passed around under the table. No bread. No apartment. No job. We had to make it together because there weren't too many other people around Sweden who could give us both what we needed. And Fay was calling me "Papa."

God must have made me one very lucky black cat. He got me out of the ghetto. Out of the Nam. Out of the hospital and walking. No, He wasn't about to let me freeze my ass off on the streets of Stockholm just when I had found the person I really needed. Come October, 1968, and I landed my first job. At fifty bucks a day! No shit. The kid was going to be a movie star. A Swedish film company, Sandrews, was making an antiwar movie by Peter Watkins, an English director. They needed a black cat—me. I've been acting and rapping all my life, so it was no big deal. Me, Whit, I'm cool. During two months of shooting, I could think of nothing but that two-thousand-dollar paycheck at the end. Now we can live!

Gladiatorerna, or *The Peace Game* in English, was finished in November, 1968. In December the three of us moved into our new flat in Skärholmen. The three of us and a Swedish cheese slicer—that's all there was when we moved in. But we moved in together. There was no more ghetto now. No more DIs. No more combat in the bush. No more murder. Nobody shooting at me. All that shit was definitely over now and I could start to live my life.

BLACK EXILE

A hell of a lot of people have helped me get where I am today. Swedes, Russians, Japanese, my black brothers. All of them had at least fifty different reasons for giving me help. I understand that, yet I'm still as thankful as any man can be who has been given back his life. But I'm especially thankful to the Japanese because they helped me as a human being. Just one man to another man and no strings attached. It was warmhearted, personal help. The Japanese didn't see me as a thing, as just a part of "the cause." Sure, the Swedes and Russians did their bit but for their own reasons. The Russians were out to peddle a little jive propaganda. And the Swedes . . . well, they have a tough time treating each other like warm-blooded people. They're not about to do anything for anybody unless it's also for "the cause." Sometimes I feel sorry for Swedes because I can see that they want to be real and down to earth. But they just can't make it, no matter how hard some of them try. Soul is what the Swedes need. There are exceptions of course, and thank God, Chiquita is one of them.

Taki. If she hadn't opened my eyes, it never would have started. I'd either be dead in one of Sam's boxes or busting my ass for the man back in a Memphis ghetto. I can never forget her. I can never really thank her.

My family? They still don't really understand what I've done. I'm their son and brother, so they love me. But they don't understand. If I had robbed a store and shot up some people back in Memphis, my family and everybody on the block would know that I'd done wrong. "He's always been a good boy, Your Honor. One of our finest young men. Go easy on him. It's only his first mistake, Your Honor." Although they'd back me, they'd know that I had committed a crime. But did they say anything when

I went off to shoot up people in Nam? Not a goddamn word but "Good luck, son. You're doing your duty." In that way, they were no different from most white American families. Americans, black and white, have forgotten how to think for themselves. They let the man on top do it all for them.

About a month ago my mother wrote me her first "Why don't you come home, son?" letter. Ma, I love you, but I'm no fool. America has nothing for me but jails and ghettos.

So I'll stay here in Sweden and try to make it as an immigrant. My job and my home are like nothing I could ever expect to have in America. But America keeps poking its big nose into my life. Sam is everywhere. A few blocks from where I live is a Honeywell factory and an Esso Motor Inn. Turn on the tube and Sam is bashing heads in Chicago . . . still burning away in Nam three years after I was there doing the same thing . . . murdering brothers in Asbury Park, Miami, Detroit, Hartford, Jackson State, Mississippi.

Jackson State. Since it happened I've read only two or three newspaper stories about that massacre of blacks. And at least one hundred stories about the murder of whites at Kent State. That's how much black lives are worth in America.

And yellow lives? Well, this morning's International Herald Tribune had a story about an eighteen-year-old Marine who got five years at hard labor for murdering eleven Vietnamese children and four women. If I go back to America, the rap is five years at hard labor plus a few more years for any other charges Sam wants to pin on me. Like writing this book is an act of disloyalty. One guy gets five years for murdering Vietnamese women and kids and I get five years for refusing to murder them.

Do I ever want to go back to America? *Nej tack.* No, thanks. I'm just not that dumb anymore.

Peace, brother.

AFTERWORD

Terry Whitmore's is one of the more remarkable memoirs to come out of the Viet Nam War. Ironically, it is among the most neglected as well. Originally published in 1971 by Doubleday under the title *Memphis-Nam-Sweden: The Autobiography of a Black American Exile*, it went out of print some two decades ago. Unquestionably, one of the reasons for this neglect is that it is about a deserter, making it a story ideologically unacceptable in this country since at least the early seventies, when a generation-long patriotic backlash began with the lionization of the POWs. The plethora of POW memoirs in that period were, by and large, affirmative of the kinds of values that Americans preferred to celebrate in themselves—perseverance through faith, courage in adversity, and the like—and very few works that presented a different picture of the Viet Nam War, novels, films, and poetry included, were welcomed in those years immediately following the ignominious "end" to the American involvement in that war in 1973. In fact, it was during this period that the preferred image of the war came to be that of the crazed vet, a view that proliferated in all media. For many years, scarcely a day went by when a news story didn't close with the information that the perpetrator of some outrage was a Viet Nam veteran, or a film or television drama didn't contain a *de rigueur* crazy, driven to mayhem by the unseen phantoms of the war.

During this time, untold numbers of novels and memoirs languished, with only a bare few, such as those by Tim O'Brien, Ron Kovic, Philip Caputo, and Michael Herr, ever seeing the light of publishing day. Those like Whitmore's that had managed to find their way into print before this ideological "big chill"—and this includes the majority of black-authored memoirs—were consigned to remainder tables and gathered dust on publishers' shelves before being pulped. The surviving copies came to occupy a tenuous place on fewer and fewer library shelves where they were less and less read, even by scholars.

Neither, however, has *Memphis-Nam-Sweden* been embraced by students of African American writing, largely due to an understandable desire by the black community to forget the Viet Nam War. After all, what was merely inglorious for most of white America was absolutely disastrous for black America. (Though certainly I recognize that for those whites, including myself, who participated or suffered losses it went much beyond the "merely inglorious.") It was this latter community, after all, which experienced the bulk of conscriptions under Project 100,000, a preponderance of its members assigned to front line duty, the highest casualty rates, and an overwhelming incidence of dishonorable and bad conduct discharges.

Thus existing on the cusps of Viet Nam literature, African American literature, and life writing, *Memphis-Nam-Sweden* has unfortunately attracted few readers in any of these fields, yet its inclusion on their recommended reading lists would appreciably add to the knowledge of all. The importance of Whitmore's story and the circumstances of the book's writing are the main subjects of this afterword, but before continuing, readers should know that Whitmore is very much alive, still, in fact, lives in Sweden, where he works as a buyer for a large company and continues to enjoy a certain international celebrity.

Memphis-Nam-Sweden itself ends, of course, with Whitmore's facing an uncertain future. Barely speaking Swedish, possessing no real marketable skills, and with few friends, he nevertheless tells us that he is about to enter a career in movies—has, in fact, just completed a role in Peter Watkins's documentary *The Peace Game*. At the same time, he reiterates his determination to remain an exile, dedicating his final chapter, "Black Exile," to indicting America for its racism. In a recent interview, he recounted that this celebrity was as much a burden as a blessing:

For a long time I was chased by every journalist around because our group [of escapees to Sweden] was the first that had been active in combat. So we were targets—especially me because I was black—for all the Swedish peace groups, to interview us and show us off. This lasted several months. The problem was, I was just trying to disappear, get on with my life, and I knew the CIA was looking for us, trying to find ways of getting us back because we were an embarrassment to Nixon. And all this attention allowed them to follow me through the journalists. I didn't want the publicity. I needed to make a living.

Eventually, he acted in several more films, most notably *Georgia, Georgia*, in which he had a major role opposite Diana Sands, and a documentary about himself called *Terry Whitmore*, which even enjoyed a brief release in the U.S. It was, in fact, Whitmore's discussion about himself in this latter film that became the basis for *Memphis-Nam-Sweden*. Because of the changing political climate mentioned above—the fragmentation of the antiwar movement caused by President Nixon's draft lottery and Vietnamization strategies—sales of the book were not good, and it stayed in print only a short time. While the American role in the war wound drearily down, Whitmore got married (though not to the woman mentioned near the end of the book) and was able through his film contacts to secure a series of jobs that made ends meet, eventually securing stable employment as a bus driver. The U.S. agencies which had earlier dogged his steps lost interest.

In the meantime, back in the U.S., his daughter (named Tonya though not so identified in the book) was growing up without having ever seen him. In addition, her mother and her mother's family had disavowed Whitmore following his desertion—"I was fine with them as long as I was a big, bad Marine but not as a deserter," he recently said—and eventually his mother, who still lives in Memphis, obtained custody and reared Tonya. Father and daughter were finally united in 1977, following President Carter's amnesty, when Whitmore returned to the U.S. for the first time in ten years as a necessary part of the repatriation process. With much trepidation, he reported to the Marine Corps base at Quantico,

Virginia. There, to his surprise, he was welcomed. "I was treated like a hero," he stated in the interview, "asked to stay in [the Marine Corps]. I had been ready for the worst, didn't know who to trust. It was weird. They even gave me the medals that had never caught up with me. I had been put up for a bronze star." Nevertheless, Whitmore wanted nothing to do with the Marine Corps's overtures, and he returned to Sweden. He married and had two sons, Jeremiah and Timothy, both of whom he intends to bring to the U.S. when they reach age eighteen, since eventual return is now in his plans following a recent divorce.

Meanwhile, *Memphis-Nam-Sweden* has taken on a life of its own. Though the book was practically forgotten in the U.S., the Japanese, of all people, remembered it, or at least its story, which was widely publicized in Japan, and in 1993 a translated edition appeared there. Following its publication, Whitmore was invited to Japan by Beheiren, the once-shadowy peace organization that originally whisked him away. Today, as an adjunct to Amnesty International they concern themselves primarily with anti-death penalty issues. In a three-month lecture tour, he spoke on their behalf at dozens of schools and, in his words, "was treated like a king all over." While in Japan, he also, with Beheiren's help, undertook an exhaustive search to locate Taki, his former girl-friend, though to no avail. In an unrelated set of events, in the U.S. work has recently been undertaken on a Hollywood screenplay based on events in *Memphis-Nam-Sweden*, a fact that serves as testimony to the power of Whitmore's story.

Its U.S. reissue, long overdue, also merits some explanation. In 1994, when I read the book, having seen it mentioned in a bibliography, I was struck first by Whitmore's comic voice—for instance, in his description of (and mostly the name) "Lynchin' Baines Johnson" and his mocking references to "Sam" (i.e., Uncle Sam) that exposes a deeply patriarchal aspect in this traditionally kind, avuncular symbol. Similarly, his method of standing outside himself acting as a semi-detached narrator commenting on his misadventures as hapless anti-hero is reminiscent of novels of the seventies and later. A good example of the emergence of this self-deprecating comic persona occurs during the incident with the Swedish women at the party (though present-day readers might wince slightly at the stereotypes and the use of words like "chick").

In addition to this distinctly contemporary comic voice, however, I also recognized that *Memphis-Nam-Sweden* was a work ahead of its time in reflecting a historical consciousness absent from virtually all Viet Nam War memoirs written during the American troop involvement. The relatively few white writers able to get memoirs published during the late sixties to early seventies dwelt very little on the larger historical and political realities of the war, tending instead to concentrate on their immediate circumstances—how they were drafted, for instance, and what happened to them while serving. Whitmore, on the other hand, is able to situate himself in relation to events like the assassination of Martin Luther King and racial unrest in the U.S. in the mid- to late-sixties. Only with the publication in 1973 of Tim O'Brien's *If I Die in a Combat Zone* did Viet Nam War memoirs begin exploring the political and historical realities in the same way that Whitmore does. Further, virtually no white-authored Viet Nam autobiography published before the end of the American involvement is able to make the connection between racism in the U.S. and in Viet Nam. Of the early memoirs only Fenton Williams's *Just Before the Dawn: A Doctor's Experiences in Vietnam* (1971) explores this link, and I think it no coincidence that Williams also is African American. Whitmore's closing chapter makes clear the similarities he sees in the situation in Viet Nam and in the U.S. in a way that simply seems unavailable to early white memoirists.

In 1995, I shared an article I was writing on the African American memoirs of the war with Kali Tal, publisher of the journal *Vietnam Generation*.[1] She urged me to try to find one or more of these writers and attempt to get their books reissued. Whitmore was easily my first choice. I wrote and then called Doubleday in an attempt to get his address, to no avail; their last address for him was dated 1971. I then got the Memphis phone book and wrote to all of the Whitmores contained there in the hope, however unlikely, that a relative of that same last name still lived there. Several months passed. I had nearly despaired of ever locating him when at 5:00 one morning the phone rang, and, in response to my groggy hello, a voice replied, "This is Terry Whitmore, calling from Sweden."

Elated (and surprised) as I was to hear from him, I soon found that the job of getting the book reissued had only begun. Whitmore himself was somewhat reluctant to undertake republication of *Memphis-Nam-Sweden* because he had compiled enough notes, he felt, to write a sequel and felt that the presence on the market of the earlier book might confuse potential readers of the second one. I convinced him (I hope correctly) that, if anything, the contrary was true, and I undertook to find a publisher. We are pleased that the University Press of Mississippi agreed that it was an important work that deserved to be in print again.

Memphis-Nam-Sweden is not only an important addition to the canons of Viet Nam War literature and American life writing but also to that of African American autobiography. Whitmore places himself squarely in this latter tradition in a number of important ways at the same time that he distinguished his story from those told in comparable white-authored books. As opposed to discussing his trauma in the manner of most white narrators, Whitmore instead stresses ways in which racial difference affected him throughout his entire story—from his home life to Marine Corps boot camp to his desertion to his final, uncertain situation as an exile in Sweden.

Whitmore reveals a good deal of his upbringing and background throughout the first quarter of the book, thus setting the stage for the same type of self-development and subsequent loss that we see in white narratives like Lewis Puller's *Fortunate Son* and Lynda Van Devanter's *Home Before Morning*. However, there is a major difference between *Memphis-Nam-Sweden* and these other narratives. Where they grew up in a world that they describe as stable and trusting, Whitmore writes of an early life that has more in common with Richard Wright's *Black Boy*. The opening pages of *Memphis-Nam-Sweden*, for instance, show a life marked by cruelty and violence, even at the hands of his own father. Against this family background, Whitmore then presents us with his initial encounters with whites, which contain that same first awareness of racial difference found in African American autobiography from Frederick Douglass to Zora Neale Hurston to Maya Angelou:

> When you're little, you never think about the fact that you're black. It just doesn't occur to you that you are colored because you're around black all the time. In school . . . you are always reading about what the white man did in history—that is, American history. But while you are reading all this shit, you never see anything about brothers. Then you begin to sense something strange. Where do we come into the picture? . . . When you reach high school, you have to go outside the neighborhood to work. This is when you really start to feel it. They do hate us. Just plain hate us. (17)

Such criticisms of their childhood universes are rare among white Viet Nam War memoirists—perhaps only Tobias Woolf's autobiographies, *This Boy's Life* and *In Pharaoh's Army*, are so revealing of the pain of family and community life. The norm is more akin to Ron Kovic, who goes to great lengths in *Born on the Fourth of July* to show how idyllic his upbringing was. Both Kovic and Whitmore elaborately reconstruct their childhoods to create a context for our later understanding of the key point of trauma in their Viet Nam experiences. However, where Kovic uses the background device to show how he, in his innocence, was duped through a patriotic upbringing into joining the Marine Corps, only to be wounded and then abandoned by his country, Whitmore—like Wright—creates a scene of familial abuse and racial hatred from which his enlistment in the Marines seems to constitute an escape.

Yet, as a result of the deep racism he encounters in the service, as well as the added problem of extremely hazardous duty in a war zone, Whitmore quickly finds himself in an even worse situation than the one he left. For instance, although he does not particularly explore the racism that he encountered in Viet Nam in the book, in our interview he told about several racially-based incidents that he witnessed there, the main one being a riot at the Freedom Hill PX in Da Nang. According to Whitmore, because of alarm at the numbers of black Marines who were "bogarting"—i.e., socializing—in the beer garden, a previously white enclave, the facilities manager took all of the soul music off of the jukebox. After protesting to no avail, the black Marines began breaking up the tables and chairs, and, when MPs were called, the incident quickly escalated into a riot in which several persons were injured and many, all black, jailed. It was only one of several such incidents that brought home to him the fact that service in the U.S. military was anything but liberating.

As a result of such experiences in Viet Nam, for Whitmore, unlike Kovic, whose crippling wounding and the aftermath are the basis of his trauma, being injured and sent to Japan is thus an additional type of escape, one that comes to represent an enhanced ideal of freedom for him, this time from the military. The ultimate trauma of Whitmore's narrative revolves not around his wounds, but rather around the price that he has to pay in order to retain this freedom, once he unexpectedly finds himself ordered back to Viet Nam instead of the U.S.

In effect, the entire last half of the book, in which Whitmore tells about his recuperation in Japan, his decision to desert, and his flight thereafter, resembles the ruminations on freedom's elusive meaning reflected in earlier African American autobiographers who had migrated North. Whether, like Douglass's, this move is an escape to actual freedom, or whether, as in Wright's or Hurston's cases, the perception of freedom is symbolic and psychological, these accounts often display an initial euphoria, followed by a succeeding period of uncertainty when the emphasis shifts from acquiring freedom to struggling to understand its limitations for African Americans. For Whitmore, the process is not different; he is initially led to believe that he will be returning home rather than to Viet Nam—a fact that represents freedom for him—and his joy increases as his body grows stronger: "Just a few more weeks and I'd be bouncing around with my little brothers and sisters. And my new daughter. The real world was getting more real all the time" (100). Yet, the realities of racial oppression are never far away, even in Japan. The incident in which he, Taki, and the other black veteran encounter the white "crackers" in the bar exemplifies the bars that he perceives to any real freedom from racial oppression as long as he remains in the Marine Corps. Ironically, it is the very home that he previously desired freedom from that he now dreams of returning to.

When Whitmore receives the shocking news that he won't be returning to the U.S. after all, but rather to his old infantry unit in Viet Nam, in a sudden rush his idea of freedom undergoes a severe dislocation: it no longer means home, as it previously had, but rather escape from being returned to Viet Nam. His primary purpose becomes to resist and escape at all costs. While Whitmore has, in fact, escaped the immediate danger facing him—returning to Viet Nam—he knows that deserting is not without its potential price. It is still not too late for him to return to Viet Nam, and he ruminates over his uncertainty. His ultimate decision is made on the basis of the probable future of a black deserter in America:

> Do I have the brains and balls to tell Sam to take his goddamn war and shove it up his big fucking white ass? . . . And if I say *no* to Sam and *no* to America and its jails, then it has to be *no* to everything I know, my family, my block, everybody. Either spend the rest of my life on the run or get lucky enough to find someplace where the man will never be kicking my black ass into doing his dirty work. (120-21)

Ultimately, as we know, he decides not to return. His escape to Sweden with the help of Beheiren is, of course, the central focus of the book, and certainly the most exciting segment. Even after arriving in Sweden, however, his situation is far from certain for he is largely without community and economic support. His doubts about the nature of freedom multiply, couched as always in the vocabulary of difference: "Sweden. Where's that? I don't know. The cat says Sweden, so we go to Sweden. Where else? Sweden sure as hell must be better than the States or Nam as far as I'm concerned, so why *not* Sweden? Well, for one thing it's a country of blond-haired, blue-eyed *white* people. So I wasn't completely without my doubts about Sweden" (168).

Memphis-Nam-Sweden ends with Whitmore a member of a new community, actively involved with the lively Stockholm international peace organization. "There was no more ghetto now," he concludes, reviewing a list of the things that had previously enslaved him. "No more DIs. No more combat in the bush. No more murder. Nobody shooting at me. All that shit was definitely over and I could start to live my life" (187). While there are indeed "no more DIs"—i.e., no more masters—there are nevertheless a different set of white controllers in his life, the equivalent of the abolitionists: the international peace movement for whom he has become a symbol, useful for a time. The original existence of the book itself is, in fact, testimony to his usefulness to the movement since he would not have had the means to get it published himself. In fact, in one of our conversations, he attested to feeling exploited after a time by the peace movement. His original collaborator on the book, an American draft resister named Richard Weber, lost interest soon after its publication and moved on, and Whitmore has neither heard from nor spoken to him since.

This matter of collaboration deserves a brief discussion because it raises questions about authorship. As Whitmore related to me, the book was transcribed directly from his testimony in the film *Terry Whitmore*. What he said there was uncoached and essentially unedited; the camera was merely trained on him, and he spoke about his experiences. This direct transcription from his testimony means, of course, that no doubt exists about authenticity. Weber made some editorial decisions, but Whitmore's unique voice unquestionably comes through. The language in the passage in which Whitmore is being feted by the Swedes gives, for example, an accurate sense of the skillful way that Whitmore establishes his voice, and the way he continually uses comic representations to undermine his own purported status as symbol for the antiwar movement. The essentially passive role that Weber played in the making of the book is further verified by the persistent presence of an error that is decidedly transcriptional in nature. In a number of passages readers might notice Whitmore voicing the essentially meaningless phrase "had it up." This, of course, is actually meant to be the phrase "hat it up," meaning to get one's hat—i.e., to leave in a hurry. Weber, as Whitmore attested to me, was unaware of this phrase's meaning and confused the "t" with a "d" when he transcribed the film, and the error thus persisted. Obviously, Weber was unwilling to change the original text even when he was unable to understand it, thus underscoring his lack of intervention.

Though Terry Whitmore continues to live in Sweden, his plans, as I suggested above, are to return to the U.S. with his sons as soon as both of them reach age eighteen. In fact, the major reason that he remained in Sweden following the 1977 amnesty was to share in the responsibility of rearing the eldest (the second being born two years later); he did not want to be an absent father, as he had been forced to be with his daughter, with whom, incidentally, he now enjoys a close relationship. Today, perhaps the most telling commentary that he can offer on the events of his life comes from his description of himself as being, above all, "patriotic." "I consider myself a loyal American," he says. "I did what I did because the country had gone wrong. Now, things are still not perfect, but a black person has a chance. I don't regret for a minute what I did—and I'd do it again—but it was because I was a loyal American that I deserted in the first place."

1. The article, entitled "MIA: The African American Autobiography of the VietNam War," appears in the Spring 1997 edition of *African American Review*.

Of the nearly 1000 memoirs of the Viet Nam War, only seven are black-authored. In addition to *Memphis-Nam-Sweden*, the memoirs by black veterans include: Eddie Wright's *Thoughts about the VietNam War* (1984), the only one published in the post-Viet Nam era, David Parks's *G.I. Diary* (1968), which is probably the best known, Samuel Vance's *The Courageous and the Proud* (1970), Fenton Williams's *Just Before the Dawn: A Doctor's Experiences in Vietnam* (1971), James A. Daly's *A Hero's Welcome: The Conscience of Sergeant James Daly versus the United States Army* (1975), and Norman A. McDaniel's *Yet Another Voice* (1975), the last two by former POWs. The novels by African American veterans number only three: George Davis's *Coming Home* (1971), A. R. Flowers's *De Mojo Blues* (1985), and John Carn's *Shaw's Nam* (1986).